Iyanla Vanzant

Faith in the Valley

Lessons for Women
on the Journey
Toward Peace

A Fireside Book
Published by Simon & Schuster

FIRESIDE
Rockefeller Center
1230 Avenue of the Americas
New York, NY 10020
Copyright © 1996 by Iyanla Vanzant
All rights reserved,
including the right of reproduction
in whole or in part in any form.

FIRESIDE and colophon are registered trademarks
of Simon & Schuster Inc.

Design by Chris Welch

Manufactured in the United States of America

20

Library of Congress Cataloging-in-Publication Data
Vanzant, Iyanla.
Faith in the valley : lessons for women on the journey to peace /
Iyanla Vanzant.
    p.   cm.
"A Fireside book."
    1. Afro-American women—Prayer-books and
        devotions—English.
2. Peace—Religious aspects—Meditations.   I. Title.
        BL625.2.V36 1996
158'.12'082—dc20   96-11894   CIP
        ISBN 0-684-80113-2

Acknowledgments

All of my work is a community effort: the community of people who love and support me, give me the inspiration to continue on the path. I salute you! I honor you! I love you!

God, my Father, my Mother, the spirit through which I live. I continue to surrender my will, my way, the fear that I won't do it right, on time, or in a way that makes people happy. Finally, I understand that God Is Enough!

The Inner Vision Spiritual Life Maintenance Team, Adara Walton, Almasi Zulu, Ebun Adelona, Erica Jackson, Gemmia Vanzant, Helen Jones, Janet Barber, Judith Hakimah, Lucille Gambrell, Mama Muhsinah Berry Dawan, and Fern Robinson, whose faith in me keeps me on target, without whose support I would miss the mark.

Joia "Louise" Jefferson, who knows everything I need to know and reminds me that I know it too! Thank you for being so willing to grow with me.

Ken and Renee Kizer, my re-birth coaches, who taught me how to breathe, who breathe with me and sometimes for me, taking me to the deepest depths of my soul, the place in me that is God. As Ken would say, "How much love can I stand?!!"

Fana Ifeula and the staff of The Other Eden, who

know how to work my kinks out and remind me to take care of the vessel.

Rev. Cochise and Vivianna Brown, who keep me cleaned out so I can go within.

Rev. Dr. Fernette Nichols, whose sermons on tape kept me grounded and in the spirit during my labor to birth this book.

Carol Ellis, an angel of God, with fingers of lightning speed, who landed in my driveway in the nick of time, to type, edit, and support the birth of this baby.

Dawn Daniels, my editor; Denise Stinson, my agent; Shaheerah Stevens, my best friend; Marge Battle, my voice of reason; you are my foundation and the fire in my spirit.

"Yu," the other half of me who keeps me praying, praising, and practicing the presence.

*Dedicated to the Memory of
the Great, Grand Diva
Miss Phyllis Hyman
and
Her Sisters
Butterfly McQueen, Rosalind Cash, Roxie Roker,
Madge Sinclair
and
My Sister-Friend
Dorothea Lois Dowell
I will always love you, my SISTAHS!*

There's a lily in the valley.

How to Use This Book

The Value in the Valley is more than just another book we can read to get hints and tips on how to improve ourselves and our lives. It is a process, with steps and principles designed to raise our consciousness and our spiritual and emotional well-being. In the book, valleys are described as, "those tight spots, dark places, uncomfortable situations we think make our lives so miserable." We all know about valleys. We have all had valley experiences: lonely, painful, confusing experiences we may believe we do not deserve, should not have, or cannot get out of. In the process of a valley experience, we often miss the lesson. A valley is a life situation designed to teach us the character traits and spiritual virtues that are undeveloped or underdeveloped during our life experiences. Valleys help us stretch, reach, and grow into our greatest potential. However, even when you know what a valley is and its potential good, you want to know what to do, how to behave in the midst of the experience. That's when you can turn to *Faith in the Valley*.

When you are trying to stay out of a valley, trying to get out of a valley, or engaging in behavior that will take you into a valley, there is probably a dominant thought raging in your mind. "Oh Lord! Why me?!!" "What the hell am I gonna do now?!!" When we are experiencing emotional stress or pressure, these thoughts become our affirmations. These are the things we say to our girlfriends when we are telling our story. They are also the things we say to ourselves when the story is too unbelievable to repeat! Unfortunately, when we are headed for or in the midst of a valley experience, we do not realize that what we think and what we say enhances the experience. The bad news is, most of the time we think and talk ourselves right into the valley. The good news is, we can use thoughts and words to get out.

Faith in the Valley is your life-support equipment. The commentaries in this book are written to support you in transforming dominant thought patterns, behaviors, attitudes, and self-defeating affirmations that can take you into the valley. Each commentary will provide you with insight about the lesson you can learn in the midst of a tragic, difficult, or frightening experience. Some commentaries will provide you with a new or different perspective on what may appear to be a problematic or confusing situation. Sometimes, a change of perspective may be all that it will take to transform a painful, frustrating, or shameful experience into an empowering growth experience. Whether you believe it or not, your thoughts and words determine your reality. When you change your mind, you can change your life.

Faith in the Valley is meant to support and enhance what you gleaned from *The Value in the Valley*, though it will work just as well if you have not read that book. The key to having faith when you are in the valley is knowing how to use the index of this book. The index in *Faith in the Valley* lists many of the things we say when we find ourselves in difficult situations. What we say is a reflection of what we think. What we think is the key to the lesson we need to learn. Because valley experiences teach us lessons, each affirmation has been ascribed to a particular valley. If you have *The Value in the Valley*, you may want to read the chapter under which the affirmation is listed in order to gain a better understanding of your particular experience. If you do not have that book, read the commentary and reflect on the message given.

At the right side of each page you will find a word or a list of words that relates to the commentary. These are lessons clues. This is what you are *growing* through. The words listed will give you a clue about the lesson you must learn or the principle you must apply to the details of your situation. In some cases it will probably be the most difficult thing you can imagine and the very thing you are resisting. DO NOT RESIST YOUR LESSONS! Resistance will push you deeper into the darkness of a valley experience. Trust Spirit! Trust yourself! Above all else, trust the process of your growth!

There will be those rare occasions when your experience is so challenging or difficult that your mind will go blank. You won't know what to think or say. You will not know what valley you are in or how you got there. In those moments you will have a particular feeling—dread, doom, hysteria, or just plain old fear. That's good enough! Turn to the index, find the word or phrase that best describes your state of mind, and read the commentary offered. This is a full service, user-friendly book. There is something here for everyone!

The commentaries offered in this book are based on spiritual laws and universal principles. If you are in a valley, these laws and principles will probably not make sense to your intellect or rational mind. In some cases, what you read in the commentary will be the last thing you want to know about. This is a signal that your resistance is rearing its ugly head, trying to keep you from getting the lesson. Life is a function of universal principles governed by spiritual laws that flow into and out of our lives. When we are unfamiliar with these laws and principles, we fight against them when they show up in our lives as experiences. We fight against them with logic, with thoughts, and with language. When we fight the universe, we end up deeper in the valley.

Because the language of the intellect and the language of spirit are not always in harmony, I offer a glossary of key terms and principles to aid in your understanding of the commentaries. When your intellect is resisting the lesson you must learn, you will believe that you do not understand the message of the commentary. I've covered that base too! Turn to the glossary, look up the lesson clue. The words listed in the glossary will provide you with a greater insight about your thinking, attitudes, and behaviors that lead to valley experiences or that will relieve a valley experience. If the lesson clue given by the commentary is not listed in the glossary, you may ascribe to it the commonly used definition. The glossary terms are provided to ensure that you have a better understanding of the universal principle or spiritual law operating in your experience. Understanding is the key to transformation. Transformation is your ticket out of the valley.

If all of the above fails to meet your needs, do not panic! Close your eyes, place the book at the center of your forehead, take a deep beath, and open to any page. Spirit always knows what you need. Rest assured that the message you open to will answer your question and point the way to a lesson. In the midst of your most difficult and challenging experience, remember—you are growing. Be gentle with yourself. Give yourself time to examine, question, and explore the principles at work and the emotions you are experiencing. Give yourself permission to fall, to get up and to do better next time. Wherever you are in your life, pray some, play some, and always have plenty of faith!

Introduction

I was ending a thirty-five-day promotional tour. Having flown all night, in a very crowded airplane, to get from Los Angeles to New Orleans, I was senseless from exhaustion and still wearing the clothes I had put on twenty-three hours earlier. I was feeling pretty ugly. After making a few telephone calls just to make sure no one wanted me to do anything for at least eight hours, I crawled into yet another hotel bed. I had only been in the bed forty-five minutes when my sister-friend staff member arrived. We decided eating made more sense than sleeping, so off we went.

Walking casually through the mall toward the food court, my companion was bringing me up to date on what was going on back at home. Then she asked me if I had heard about Phyllis. She had been found dead the day before. Beyond exhaustion there is numbness. In a state of numbness, the news that your sister-friend has left her body is called "the valley." I told my companion to shut her mouth. It was the only logical response to the feeling of pain, fear, confusion, and loss that descended over my body. I felt the pain, but I knew to go there would mean I would be subject to going crazy in a New Orleans shopping mall. I surrendered the thought. Actually, I shut down and continued the search for something I could tear apart with my teeth.

With a few morsels of food in my body, I moved out of numbness and back to exhaustion so that I could ask the question: *"Why?"* Why is not the appropriate question to ask when you are in the valley, because a mind in pain will reject everything except what it wants to, needs to hear. If the mind does not find what it needs and wants, it will ask why ad infinitum. After I asked and rejected all plausible explanations, I engaged in appropriate valley behavior: I cried.

Crying is a good thing to do in the valley because it clears the channels of communication. Crying purifies and cleanses. I once read about a scientific experiment which demonstrated that there are 38 toxic chemicals in a tear of sadness, while only one toxin exists in a tear of joy. As you cry in sadness, fear, or confusion, you cleanse the body and spirit of the toxins which cloud the mind and prevent it from accepting the truth. Once I had sufficiently purified, I asked the more appropriate question when one has fallen into a valley: "What is the lesson here?" In the quiet, undeniable way of spirit, the answer came. "She did not pass the test. The choice was hers to make." As my mind could now accept the truth, I fell into a peaceful sleep.

No matter who you are, you will have a valley experience at some time in your life. It just "be's" that way. For some, a valley will be a time of great fear, confusion, and, probably, emotional turmoil. For others, it may be a grave inconvenience or a time of seemingly endless struggle. You may whine, complain, shut down, or beg God for mercy. The truth is, you will only get what you need to grow. You are not being punished, you are being fortified!

In a great holy book of the Eastern tradition, the Bhagavad Gita, there is a passage which reads, "You will be tested! What if the Creator has a great task for you to perform and you are unprepared? Your tests come to ensure that you will be prepared when your time comes to serve." A valley is a testing experience which prepares you for greater service. Serving the Creator is what life is all about. Many of us, in the quest "to do" and "to get," forget service. We have not been taught that service means to "be" the embodiment of the Creator, actualizing all the attributes of the Creator as what we are. The Creator is life, truth, love, harmony, balance, principle, and peace. In living we become so busy "doing" we forget to "be." Humans doing are not human beings.

The wise woman, mother, sister, and stage diva Beah Richards once told me, "You are a human being, which means you lack no thing essential to your survival. You are whole, complete and loved just as you are. That is how I love you." This is also how God, the Creator loves us. Just as we are is the physical embodiment of God Itself. What we look like, what we do, what we have, does not alter what God made us to be. Living in a doing-made world, confronted by rules, laws, and expectations which force us to do, has a way of wiping the knowledge of our divinity right out of our memory. We become indoctrinated to a process of struggle, conflict, restriction, and denial based on what we do, what we get, and how we look to others who try to out-do and out-get us. Then we get mad. We get mad at the people who participate in the struggle, conflict, restriction, and denial with us. Then we get mad at our self for having the experience. Some of us go so far as to get mad at God for not helping us "do" better.

What we call living or trying to live is not life! God is life! God is not in conflict or struggle with anyone about anything. God is not restricted or restrictive. God cannot deny Itself. God perfects! This perfecting presence is always with us at the core of our being, even when we are in the valley.

With my father and mother gone from active living, it has been easy for me to turn to God. I had nowhere else to go! Then I realized the nowhere means, "now here." Even after I had this revelation, there were days when I got very busy "doing"; times when I went into fear; moments, sometimes weeks, of total confusion. I have even had experiences of temporary insanity. These were my valleys. It took a while for me to realize that all testing experiences fortify my faith, strengthen my character, and open my soul to the perfecting presence.

I have learned to breathe through those testing times. I am no longer afraid to let go, to give up control and allow spirit to work in my life. In those now-rare moments when I do forget to breathe or how to let go, I grab a book. A book of spiritual truth which will jar my memory back to my divinity, the truth of who I am. This offering is something for you to grab and hold onto if you should happen to forget what else to do. Keep it near at all times. Hold it tightly in the testing times. And, when all else fails, act on faith!

I love you just as you are!

Iyanla

The Valley of Light

*Teaches us the lesson of stillness, through the
imposition of a state of solitude and silence which
forces us to take a look at ourselves.*

Let us learn to be still and let the Truth speak through us: to be still and know that the inner light shines.

—THE SCIENCE OF MIND

LIFE DOES WHATEVER is necessary to mold us into shape and prepare us for greatness. It does not always look or feel this way. Instead, what we experience in life seems difficult, painful, unnecessary. Just for a moment, think of the stones which were used to build the pyramids and the gems which fashion the Crown Jewels. Imagine how the stones were dug from the quarry and then hammered and chiseled into shape. Realize that each stone or gem had to be perfectly shaped before it could be set in its appropriate place. Recognize that once the pyramids were built and jewels cast into the Crown, they have never been disturbed, nor have they shifted, fallen, or crumbled.

Somehow life teaches us to understand that God has a perfect plan for us; according to that plan, we must be molded and shaped prior to being cast into our perfect place. When we truly recognize that there is a master plan, we can welcome any tool that comes to prepare us to behold our perfect place. When we are shaped and molded by life according to God's perfect plan, the world is amazed and blessed by our beauty, and longevity.

Get prepared to be prepared!

RIGHT WHERE YOU are is where you need to be. Don't fight it! Don't run away from it! Stand firm! Take a deep breath. And another. And another. Stop beating up on yourself. Don't blame anyone else. Breathe. Now, ask yourself: Why is this in my world? What do I need to see? To know about myself through this situation? Breathe again. Now, ask God:

Blessed and Divine Father/Mother, heal me of whatever thought or belief has contributed to the cause of this experience. Bring me the lesson of this experience lovingly and gently. Keep my mind and heart open that I may know the truth. Open my eyes that I may recognize your will. Thank you, God.

Now breathe. Don't you feel better already?

God is right here, right now!

BAD THINGS ARE going to happen. Painful, ugly, frustrating events are going to take place. There is no way around getting your feelings hurt, having your ego bruised, your trust weighed, your heart broken. Life has its ups and downs. If you are living, you are bound to trip or fall every now and then. There is not much you can do while you are going through your challenges and difficulties, but there is something you can remember that will make it a bit easier to bear.

The same God that was good yesterday is good today. The same God that loved you last week, loves you today. The same powerful, almighty, all-knowing God that saved you, comforted you, guided you the last time you needed it, will save, comfort, and guide you today. Right where you are, in the midst of trouble, take a moment to be loved, comforted, guided, by the good God who knows exactly what you need. God is present. God's presence is called grace.

Live in the presence of God's grace.

WHEN MY HUSBAND left, I thought I had been a bad wife. Then my son went to jail, and I knew I had been a bad mother. When my best friend and my mother died, I slipped face first into being a bad person. How was I supposed to figure it all out?

All women fall into the valley. Some fall deeper than others. The valley is a lonely place. A dark and confusing pit in the center of your brain. You can't figure it out. You can't get out. You've got a black hole in your life into which everything you've ever really wanted seems to fall, into the valley. I once thought it was cruel and inhumane punishment; now I know it is a reward. The stronger and more gifted you are, the deeper and eventually more rewarding is the valley experience.

We all have our lessons to learn in life. Most of us fail to learn unless we are in some kind of pain. The valley is your pain. The valley gets your attention. The valley lets you know what you are doing and why you just might want to try something new. The bad thing is that no one can warn you a valley is coming. You must pay attention to what is going on in your life! The good thing is that once you've been there, in enough pain, you figure it out. People begin to notice. "Hey, what's up with you?" "You look different." "Did you change your hair or something?" You haven't changed your hair, your mind has changed. You have learned a very valuable lesson. When you can't, FAITH CAN!

Faith makes the day and paves the way!

DEAR SELF,
Guilt says,
"There is something wrong with what I have done."
Shame says,
"There is something wrong with me."
You can eliminate guilt by making amends
for what you have done.
You cannot eliminate shame
until you know and believe,
"All that God is, I Am."
God is truth, mercy, wisdom, strength, forgiveness,
peace, order, justice, and love.
What have you got to be ashamed of?

God is not ashamed of me. Neither am I.

YOU CAN'T SHRINK into greatness. When you reflect on the things you have done and not done, there is a tendency to beat up on yourself. We criticize, judge, and condemn ourselves much more severely than the world could or would. In response to this self-flagellation, we shrink away from doing or attempting to do. You cannot shrink into your greatness! We must use our past as a road map, a key, that unlocks our capabilities by giving us understanding of our frailties. The past simply tells us what we can do, cannot do, what we need to work on or work out.

You must know every intricate detail of yourself. Your past is like an X-ray machine. Once you see what is there, don't shrink, shine! Now you know, which means you can take appropriate steps toward healing and correction. Don't fight with yourself! Accept who you are now and all you've done. Then give yourself a big hug and kiss. You've been through a lot. A little loving tenderness could be what you need right now.

I love to love me.

REPETITION IS THE mother of skill. If you do something enough you get good at it. When what you are doing is good for you, it is pleasurable, and you want to do it often, getting better and better at it. However, when what we do is not pleasurable, we fight against it, resisting the discomfort, and avoiding the lesson we may need to learn.

When unwanted situations repeat themselves in our lives, there is something we have missed. There is a blind spot in our consciousness, something we can't see and don't know yet. Repeat performances of bad productions will continue coming up as an experience in our lives. We go through it again, again, wracking our brains, grasping at straws, trying to figure out how we got here and how we can get out.

Those repetitive issues which cause us displeasure are just like the things Mother told us over and over. We didn't want to hear them; we ignored what she said. In the end, we saw Mother's point. Finally, we realized, she only wanted us to be better; well, so does life. When you find yourself in the same situation repeatedly, do not fight against what you are going through. It is in your own best interest to look for the lesson and cultivate the skill, to do a new thing, in a new way.

I Am, I Am, I Am, I know I Am, learning something very valuable.

LITTLE PROBLEMS IN life are like a pop quiz which will determine whether or not you are in touch with your feelings; whether you have learned to trust yourself or will continue to move along mindlessly in your old ways. Many of us ignore the little things, those uneasy rumblings, because we can't believe it is happening . . . again. We step willingly into bad situations, because we don't want to believe we could be "wrong" about them. Yet we readily believe we could be "wrong" about what we feel. If you don't believe yourself, when you don't trust what you feel, it means you are in doubt. Doubt will push you headfirst into a valley.

Sometimes an uneasy feeling will be the normal fear or doubt associated with doing things that are different or new. At other times, it will be life warning you to get still, pay attention, remember what happened the last time you didn't pay attention to yourself, and act accordingly.

Here is a clue about life's little warnings: monsters don't have shadows! You will never see the monster coming. It will descend upon you before you recognize it. If you are feeling uneasy for no apparent reason, it means you are being quizzed about something you are adequately equipped to handle, based on past experience. Whether you pass or fail the quiz is a reflection of how much you know about and trust yourself.

Trust what you feel!

33

WHEN YOU GET the urge to stay home, be alone, pull back, or shut down, it is probably your spirit urging you to take a rest. Do not ignore it! Honor yourself by taking some time out. Take a day away. There may be something very important going on within you that you need to know about. You must get quiet in order to hear it. The job will be there, and people will simply have to understand; what can be done today can also be done tomorrow. All duties and responsibilities can wait. Your spirit cannot!

I have often heard people say, "I need a break!" but they never take one. I know it is no coincidence when these same people break their foot or when their car breaks down, forcing them to "be still." Often we think there is something wrong with us when we "don't want to be bothered." So we keep moving and doing. Spirit knows what we need and provides it for us. Yet when incidents force us into a needed solitude, we reach outward rather than within. Rest, Stillness, Solitude, Introspection, Reflection, are spiritual vibrations. They keep us from breaking down, falling apart, and being forced into a living deficiency.

Today is a spiritual health day!

DEAR GOD,

Today, I want to be still, to listen, to hear, and to know. Today, I want to see and know myself as a reflection of You. Today, God, I want the stillness of Your love to shower me in the light of perfect peace, that I may go forth stronger, wiser, in readiness to do Your perfect will. Today, God, I want to be still with You.

Lord, keep me still today! Take away all that makes me race and worry and fear and doubt and rush away from myself. Take away the need to do, be, have, know, want anything other than the grace of Your love. Show me myself today, Lord. Show me Your perfect child, on a divine mission, fulfilling Your perfect purpose, in a divine way. And, Lord, help me understand You and me, how we can work together in stillness to create new life.

Today, Lord, I am willing to be still in Your arms, still in Your light, still in Your love. I am willing to see You in me and release all that is not. I am willing to know You in my life, to preserve You in my heart, to open myself to more of You as what I am. In stillness I see You. In stillness I accept You. In stillness I feel You. Lord, let me be still, just for today. Thank You, God.

Today, move in stillness.

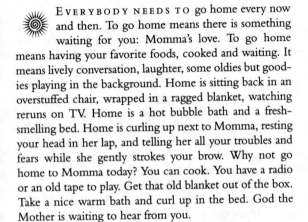 EVERYBODY NEEDS TO go home every now and then. To go home means there is something waiting for you: Momma's love. To go home means having your favorite foods, cooked and waiting. It means lively conversation, laughter, some oldies but goodies playing in the background. Home is sitting back in an overstuffed chair, wrapped in a ragged blanket, watching reruns on TV. Home is a hot bubble bath and a fresh-smelling bed. Home is curling up next to Momma, resting your head in her lap, and telling her all your troubles and fears while she gently strokes your brow. Why not go home to Momma today? You can cook. You have a radio or an old tape to play. Get that old blanket out of the box. Take a nice warm bath and curl up in the bed. God the Mother is waiting to hear from you.

Mother, I'm coming home.

IN ANCIENT TIMES, it was believed that little boys needed special protection in life. Boys were covered in blue. Blue represents the heavens. When you covered a baby boy in blue, you were providing him the energy and protection of God. It was also thought that girls did not require, or even "deserve," the same protection. Girls were fragile. Girls were meant to serve and be protected by boys. Girls were covered in pink to represent their sweet, fragile nature.

As silly as this may sound, it represents the dominant thought pattern of our culture. Boys are entitled to the world of God. Girls get ignored, pushed aside, abused, or abandoned by the boys. Don't they deserve special recognition themselves? You can begin today.

Remind your little girl, it is not what she wears, it is not the ribbons in her hair. It is not the color of her skin, the ruffles on her panties, or the neighborhood she lives in. Little girls are also expressions of God; this makes them worthy to the world. Little girls are valuable because they are; not because of what they do, what they have, or what they want to be. Little girls bring forth the grace of life in their smiles, laughter, questions, and expressions. There is a little girl in you. Have you loved her today? Have you hugged or kissed her today? Have you told her how special she is, how valuable she is, and how much you appreciate and honor her? Have you told the little girl in you how beautiful she is just because she is!

It is safe for you to be a little girl.

I'm all alone. I don't have nobody.

Fear,
Faith

 NO ONE WANTS to be alone when things are not going well. Whether we fall or are pushed into one of life's difficulties, we don't want to be there on our own. In the darkness of trouble, we reach out for someone to help us. If we are lucky, they can't! They may want to, but there is simply no way anyone else can learn our lessons with us or for us.

If you are a slow learner, you might get mad at friends you think should help but don't. You may become disillusioned or resentful of the family members who always call on you but never answer when you call. If you are a spiritual special-education candidate, you may complain or whine and stamp your feet, declaring, "Why me?" "This is not fair!" "I can't take this anymore!" Oh, you can take it! We can always take the dark, lonely, frightening valley experience, because we have no other choice!

Your blessings have your name on them; so do your lessons! Your greatest blessing appears before you, cleverly disguised as your most difficult challenge, as your greatest obstacle, or as an extremely negative experience you are forced to handle all by yourself. What a blessing! What a blessed opportunity to face the truth, forgive yourself and others, practice faith, develop trust, be still, and know, "Right where I am, God is!"

I Am not alone! I Am learning!

WHERE DID WE get the idea that we must do it "all" alone? There is a guardian angel called the "Grace of God" waiting to serve us whenever we have need. So many of us struggle through life completely ignorant of the fact that the "Love of God" is sufficient protection, support, and supply under all circumstances. Far too many of us take on more than we need or want to, and by doing so, we get in God's way.

At all times, no matter what situation may confront us, "grace" is our escape route. With a long, deep breath, relaxation of the stomach muscles, and the silent affirmation "By the grace of God," we are given a clear mind and divine guidance. Often this brief exercise provides us with a new insight or renewed strength. Sometimes it lets us know that there is absolutely nothing we can do, and even this is okay. In a state of not being able to help ourselves, God's love surrounds us. This love brings us peace, contentment, and a silent strength. It brings us the ability to say no without guilt; the presence of mind to "let go" without fear; more importantly, it reminds us that with faith we can do all things.

The next time pressure, responsibilities, demands, or expectations push you to the point of overwhelm, invoke the grace; surrender to love. And let the blessings fall as they may.

By the grace, with the love of God, I Am.

———

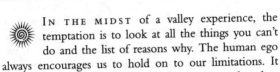 IN THE MIDST of a valley experience, the temptation is to look at all the things you can't do and the list of reasons why. The human ego always encourages us to hold on to our limitations. It always seems easier to look at what is wrong rather than stretch to what could possibly be just fine. If we would see things as perfectly fine, just the way they are, no matter what they are, we might realize we are fine too. For some of us, this is a far stretch. But that's fine, and so are you.

If you are alive, that's fine. If you have a vision for tomorrow, that's fine. People may be pressuring you or upset with you. That's fine. You may be upset, afraid, angry, and anxious; that's just fine. You will get over it. If you can remember a time, any time when you were in a fix, a jam, a place in your life you did not want to be, that is fine. Now, can you remember that you are not where you were anymore? Or realize you made it through . . . somehow? Haven't you always gotten what you needed? And when you didn't, you made it through anyway. Perhaps things did not work out the way you wanted, but they are turning out. Most important of all, they are turning out to be just fine.

No matter what, it's fine.

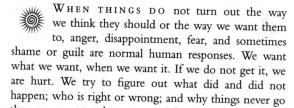 WHEN THINGS DO not turn out the way we think they should or the way we want them to, anger, disappointment, fear, and sometimes shame or guilt are normal human responses. We want what we want, when we want it. If we do not get it, we are hurt. We try to figure out what did and did not happen; who is right or wrong; and why things never go the way we want them to go. Often, we do not realize that the moment we try to make something happen, the pain begins.

Reflect on the number of times you have asked for something and gotten it, only to realize it did not make you feel the way you thought it would. Now, reflect on those situations when things did not go your way and still turned out to be just fine. In the moment of disappointment, it may be hard to remember the good things gone bad and the bad things gone good. It is much easier to feel bad or get mad, which is exactly why we must be on guard and not do it.

There is a divine order in the universe of life which operates to protect our best interests, even when we cannot see it. Divine order will save us from ourselves. Order will bring peace. If we would "order" the brain to stop chattering, clamoring, and creating drama, the pain we think we are in would be transformed to an orderly flow of events. In the flow of life, divine order often brings our good at the perfect time in the perfect way.

Faith transforms confusion into order.

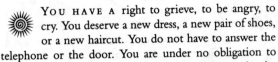 YOU HAVE A right to grieve, to be angry, to cry. You deserve a new dress, a new pair of shoes, or a new haircut. You do not have to answer the telephone or the door. You are under no obligation to show up unless you want to. If you want to stay under the covers, or sit naked in the middle of the floor and eat grapes, go right ahead and do it. Never be so responsible for the world that you forget to be responsible to yourself.

Confusing, tragic, painful events will come and go. These events cause shifts in our minds and upheavals in our hearts for which we need time to grieve, heal, understand, and accept. It is a process of taking care of one's self. While the brain is clearing, the heart mending, the body healing, it may mean taking a break from the regular routine, and moving away from the routine people. Give yourself permission to do whatever is necessary to take care of you. Take a walk. Have a cry. Break a glass. Write a letter. Pull your dress up over your head! Go ahead, do whatever it takes to help you feel better.

Today, just take care of yourself!

Some people are important because they make themselves so.
Some people are important because other people make them so.
Other people are important because God makes them so.
They are the people who never brag or boast or know so.
—Rev. Dr. Fernette Nichols

God makes an important difference!

SOME PEOPLE ARE compelled by the theoretical desire to live a spiritual life. These people are curiosity-seekers who will try a little of this and a little of that, never sticking to anything long enough to see if it actually works. Those who are theoretically spiritual read the books and know the language; they attend the workshops so they know what to do. However, in crisis they will panic. In disappointment they will criticize and condemn. In fear they will lie. In anger they become unforgiving and judgmental. You see, theory alone does no good. You must practice the principles in order to realize the truth. The more consistent and devoted the practice, the greater the realization and demonstration of truth.

The other telltale sign of a theoretical spiritualist is that they get full fairly quick. They have forgiven enough. They are grateful enough. They have given enough praise. The Christ said we should forgive seventy times seven. We must praise unceasingly; we must be grateful beyond measure. Isn't it interesting that those of us who have difficulty giving ourselves to one thing can measure when we have done enough of something else?

*Today, I will give more, do more,
have more of one thing.*

THERE DOESN'T HAVE to be anything *wrong* with you to want to do better. You don't have to be broke or brokenhearted, hated or hateful to be in search of a better way. For some reason, we seem to feel where we are is as far as we can go. We have convinced ourselves not to look for a better way; a new path is an admission that something is not good about where we are. This is simply not true.

"I can do better" does not translate to "I am doing bad." It is actually a recognition of the unlimited potential of the human spirit. The spirit within us has the ability to grow beyond all time, space, and physical matter in response to our receptivity. Our job is to remain open, to never be so comfortable where we are as to believe we cannot continue to grow. Most important of all, even when we believe we are the best we can be, we can do more, learn more, be more, by teaching what we know to somebody else.

There's more to me than this.

NO MATTER WHAT situation you find your-self in; no matter how many times you promised yourself, "This will never happen to me again"; no matter how old you are, how "stupid" you feel; no matter what you think other people will think about you, say about you; no matter how bad you feel, how frightened you are; resist the urge to beat up on yourself, and love yourself.

Go ahead, love yourself right now. Touch yourself. Give YOU a big hug. Gather yourself up in your arms and rock yourself for a little while. Now say something encouraging to you. Try, "I will always love you, no matter what." Tell yourself, "You're okay with me, no matter what!" If you are really sincere, you will probably hit a raw nerve. When you do, you will cry. Good! Love has a way of touching the core of the being, and breaking it down to the basic element: love. You can love yourself into and out of anything. Perhaps you are where you are because you need a little love. So before you try to figure out what to do, love yourself. Nobody can do it better than you!

Love appears as new experiences.

A SPIRITUAL BROTHER and friend, Rocco Errico, explained embarrassment to me this way: It's like spilling milk. When you spill the milk, God throws you a rag and says, "Here! Clean up your mess!" The rag is truth, faith, discipline, obedience to do what you know you must, what is in your best interest. Sometimes we are courageous enough to face the messes we create in our lives and clean them up. At times we leave one mess and go create another one. When we do, God doesn't get angry. S/He says, "Here's the rag; tell the truth, admit your faults, make amends; clean it up." If we spill the milk again and again and again, God will continue to throw us the rag and wait for us to clean it up. Often, we expect God to clean up the mess for us. We beg and plead and cry. God simply waits, because God knows, when we get tired of cleaning up the mess, we will stop spilling the milk!

I will clean up after myself.

HARD WOOD. HARD-BOILED eggs. Hard nails. These are good things in life. Hard knocks, hard head, hard heart, hard bed, hard life, is not what we want to look forward to every day. Yet most little girls are indoctrinated to believe it's hard in the world and that's that! My mother told me, "If you make your bed hard, you have to lie in it." So my hard head resulted in many hard knocks. And as I accepted all the hard times, I became hard-hearted. But life is good, and one day I asked, "Why, oh why, Momma, do I have to stay in the hard bed?" It was then that I realized that each day is a new opportunity for a new beginning and a new way. If I stopped thinking hard, acting hard, feeling hard, looking hard for something hard to happen, maybe things would ease up . . . just a little.

I can hardly wait to see the good coming my way.

WHAT'S THE MATTER with you?!! Here you are doing things the way you do them, the only way you know how, the way "they" taught you to do them. Yet for some reason, it just doesn't seem to work.

Look at you! There you go again! Doing that, the way you think you should, the way "they" told you you should, and look at what is happening!

I can't believe you did that! Not again! Not now! But you did, didn't you? Now what are you going to do?

If I were you, I would simply "be."

Face it, no matter what you do, someone is not going to be happy. In addition to that, there is no right or wrong in doing. There simply is what "is." Whatever you do, you will continue to do it, the way you do it, until you "grow" into doing something else. You cannot be wrong. You can only be who you are, doing what you do, in order to become better.

Whatever you do is exactly what you need to do in order to learn what you need to know. As you learn, you become better at what you do. When you get better, you will do a new thing, and someone else will still not be happy. The good news is, no matter what you do, you will learn how to do it better; or you will learn what not to do in order to be better. Now there is absolutely nothing wrong with that, is there?

I am doing, learning, and growing.

The Valley of Understanding

Teaches us to accept ourselves, other people, and situations as they are, not as we want them to be. Understanding is the ability to get underneath the thing and stand in the truth of what it is.

*B*etrayal teaches that you can survive anything. All the things you thought you couldn't handle, you can.

—OPRAH WINFREY

THE QUICKEST WAY to turn a bad situation into a blessing is to get excited! Things may not look so good right now. You may even doubt your ability to hold up under the pressure or the scrutiny. It's all okay! You can still choose to be excited! Excitement is the opposite of anxiety. It brings a new energy into any situation. Excitement gives you power and puts you in charge of what you do.

Just imagine how you will feel when the situation is over. Think about what you will do with the knowledge and experience you are gaining. Think about the stories you can tell, the people you can assist, the fact that you will know what to do if you are ever in this situation again. Is that exciting?

In any situation, you have the right, power, and ability to choose your experience. Old habits and negative thought patterns will be the first to show up, but we can choose a new way in which you affect the outcome. Rather than slipping into fear, resentment, or anger, you can get excited! Be excited that this has come to an end. Be excited that you are equipped to handle it! Be excited that life is trusting you to do the right thing! Be excited that you will do your best, no matter what happens.

I'm so excited!

THE PAIN WE experience in life is not always physical. People hurt in many ways for many reasons. Unfortunately, we are programmed at a very early age to take something or to do something to make the pain go away. The taking or doing will often give us temporary relief. It usually does not root out the cause of the pain. As a result, we do what we must in the moment to find relief, and in doing so ignore the growing malignancy which initially caused the pain.

The physical, mental, or emotional shift we call pain is actually a marvelous teaching tool. When you hurt, you become acutely aware that something you are doing, or have done, is not good for you. When you are in pain, a weakened state, you want to reach out; however, life is telling you to reach within. A habitual behavior pattern, a persistent thought pattern, a response to an event or series of events is usually at the root of the pain. If you hurt long enough and hard enough, you just might be prompted to stop participating in those activities which create the pain.

No matter what kind of pain we experience in life, see it as a shift toward something better. Remember, you are equipped to handle it. Resist the urge to get temporary relief. As you learn and grow, you will realize the greater the pain, the greater the growth. The greater the growth, the less is the likelihood that you will do anything to knowingly hurt yourself ever again.

OUCH! I Am growing through this!

MOST OF US probably couldn't stand having all of our problems solved at one time. There would be so much light and power, we would be blown away. Some of us would be so frightened, we would constantly peer over our shoulder, waiting for the disaster to come. In life, we see our problems as one great big mountain. In order to move the mountain, you have to chip away one grain of sand at a time.

At certain points, you will have to move the same grain of sand several times. As you repeat the same thing over and over, you will get clear about what you do. Some parts of the mountain will fall away with very little effort on your part. Maybe that part had nothing to do with you. It got mixed in with your stuff along the way. Some parts of the mountain will resist your efforts; they will not be moved. Don't get stuck. When you are standing in front of the mountain, resist the feeling of overwhelm. Move the piece of sand closest to you; that is easy to pick up. Pay attention to how you move it. Don't forget to celebrate yourself for every grain of sand that you move.

I can do this! One step at a time! One day at a time!

WHEN YOU GET through whatever it is you are going through, you are going to be much better off. You will have firsthand knowledge of what works for you and what does not. You will have a new assessment of your strengths and capabilities. You will have greater insights about the people in your life. Perhaps you will have trimmed away some fluff, released some unnecessary baggage. In the midst of a challenge, our eyes are opened, our minds blown to new levels of awareness. When you get through this, you are going to be something else . . . a better, stronger you!

Just another growth experience, blessing me today.

YOU DID EVERYTHING you were supposed to do, the way you were supposed to do it. You even did it on time. You put your best foot forward, utilized all of your resources, followed all the rules, and things still didn't turn out as you planned. Well, don't be alarmed, angry, or frustrated; it happens to the best of us. The challenge is to realize and accept that we simply cannot see everything.

All of us have a blind spot, a weak area, a point of vulnerability of which we are simply unaware. There will be those instances in which our best efforts are for naught. When our deepest desire goes up in smoke. This will not always mean we did it wrong; it simply means we did not see it right. When we are blindsided by tragedy, disaster, or disappointment, the lesson becomes knowing that our best is always good enough, no matter what the outcome appears to be.

I should have seen it coming, but I didn't.

WHEN THINGS HAPPEN that upset or frighten children, they run away. When they do "bad things," they hide. Children believe "bad things" will kill them, or if they do bad things they will lose love. If there is no one around to support, protect, or reassure children, they find ways, mentally and emotionally, to escape the punishment they might receive.

When children grow up, they realize the bad things did not kill them, yet adults will still find ways to escape unpleasant or frightening experiences. Mentally we make excuses, lay blame, find fault to escape the "bad thing" that has happened or that we have done. Emotionally we create defenses, crying, swearing, lying, striking out to cover our fear or shame. It is a reflection of the little child inside trying to run away and hide.

In the midst of your most troubling time, difficult challenge, frightening experience, know that you can feel bad and recover. It is not the pain, fear, shame, or guilt which will "kill" you; it is your attempt to run away that will. When we run from our challenges, we kill off our power. We strangle our strength. We suffocate our character. We assassinate our character and the ability to grow. "Be still and know . . . no matter what, you will survive." Chances are, if you reassure yourself, just a bit, you will grow faster than you imagined.

I shall not run or hide.

WE MUST AVOID the tendency to compare ourselves with anyone else. We must resist the urge to compare where we are and what we are doing against the strides or failures of another. Comparison of self to others feeds self-doubt. Self-doubt grows into self-defeat. My grandmother always said, "Mind your own business!" I now understand what she meant in a completely different light.

Your growth is your business, and it has nothing to do with how anyone else is growing. When you do the best you can, where you are, with what you have, it does not matter what anyone else is doing. The time spent watching and comparing yourself to others is time that could be spent developing your skills, perfecting your craft, creating your visions of the future. What you are doing is your own business. When you pay attention to it, it will ultimately pay off for you—not the people you are watching.

I can grow at my own divine pace.

A COURSE IN *Miracles* states, "You are never
angry for the reason you think." This implies that
there is an underlying reason for our anger. If we
extend this theory to any negative emotion—fear, shame,
guilt, betrayal, rejection, disappointment—the same principle applies: we are never upset for the reason we think
we are; there is always something else going on.

One challenging experience in life will always trigger
our old stuff. That stuff will show up as more confusion,
greater difficulty, more pain. In the midst of our challenges, we must take a moment to ask, "What am I really
feeling?" An honest inquiry will undoubtedly produce,
"I'm not good enough, smart enough, pretty enough,"
which all boils down to, "I'm not enough." If this personal
lie is at the core of your challenge, ask yourself, "When
was the first time I heard this? Who said this to me?"
When you identify the person, forgive him or her. You
must forgive that person for crippling your self-concept,
self-image, self-value. After you forgive that person or
those people, forgive yourself for believing them.

Forgiveness heals old wounds. Forgiveness removes us
from the shadows of the past. Forgiveness helps us understand where we are, how we got there, how to shut the
door and not return.

There is something here I must forgive!

DEAR GOD,

Have mercy on me. Your mercy, Your grace, Your love, are my strength. Your mercy clears my mind, renews my soul, reminds me I am the loved child of a loving Father who knows my needs before I ask. Your mercy kindles love in my heart, wisdom in my mind, life in my human being. Have mercy on me.

Dear God, forgive me. I know I have not always lived according to Your word. I have not always honored Your will, but You love me anyway. Today I confess to You my frailties as a human, and ask that You send Your Spirit to heal me of the thoughts, habits, and beliefs that keep me from the full realization of You in my being and life. Forgive me for anything I have done consciously or unconsciously to push You out of my life.

Dear God, restore me. Restore me to the state of peace in my mind, love in my heart, balance in my soul with which You created me. Restore my faith in myself and my life. Restore discipline in my spirit and my deeds. My desire is to know and serve You with all my heart and soul, that I may have my eyes opened to the miraculous nature of Your being.

For this, to You, I give thanks.

I Am forgiven! I Am restored through God's mercy.

FOR MANY OF us, it is hard to believe that we have been chosen. Our lives, the circumstances and conditions in which we live, make it very difficult to believe that we have a special purpose, a special place in God's heart. Even though it is hard to believe, it is true. The chosen have many tests and trials. They also have the chosen ability.

Just for today, allow yourself to believe you have been chosen. All of the experiences you have had were your training ground. If you are still here, you made it through. Every experience you thought was a bad experience was simply a test. Guess what? You passed! All the times you were down, you got up. All the things you could not do, got done. Everything you thought you messed up worked out anyway. Why? Because you have been chosen, and the chosen have a very special ability. It's called God.

Remember that you have been chosen!

———

SPIRIT IS SELF-CORRECTING. If you continue to do that which you know not to be good for you, eventually it will cause you so much pain, you will stop. If you continue to eat, drink, smoke, spend without a budget, stay in toxic relationships, you will become so miserable you will find the strength, courage, willpower to rehabilitate yourself.

Spirit really is self-correcting. The longer you do a thing, the better you get at it. The more you pray, the faster your answer will come. If you increase your practice of meditation, the calmer and stiller your mind will be. If you read more, reassure yourself more, support, nurture, and honor yourself more each day you will feel better. Instead of feeling anger or confusion, you will be clearer, more focused, and peaceful. The self-correcting spirit in you will make the best of what you do more of—more destruction, greater pain; more construction, greater peace, pleasure, and plenty.

You will do it until you understand what you are doing.

IN THE REALM of human experiences, death seems to be the one thing that has the power to make us feel powerless. Whether it is the end of a physical life or the end of a situation which has meant a great deal to us, death, the end, seems so final. It may seem that way, but it doesn't have to be that way. In reality, death is simply another way the nature of life calls upon us to shift, change perspective, reach, and grow to new heights of consciousness.

It may take a little time to process the body and mind through the emotion of the experience. However, once that occurs, there is a power within the spirit capable of helping us make the shift. In the face of death, an end, or a separation, we have the spiritual power to make peace, continue communication, forgive, release, share, and find closure. Writing a letter to the departed one, letting them know you miss them and think about them is an excellent process. Mailing the letter is optional. Communicating your thoughts and feelings provides the healing.

You can mentally speak to the person. In this way you can say whatever is in your heart, all the things you did not have the opportunity or courage to say in person. More important, when we turn to spirit, the consciousness shifts an unwanted ending to spiritual closure. Closure enables you to release. With closure we can find the strength to accept; and understand, and the strength to recover from the experience and move on.

You have the power to bring closure to this experience.

REMEMBER WHAT HAPPENED the last time you second-guessed yourself, or let people talk you out of what you had decided to do? Have you forgotten what happened when you changed your mind back and forth six times and settled on doing what you thought would make "them" happy? Don't you remember what happened the last time you didn't pay attention to yourself, didn't trust yourself? You ended up in trouble!

For most of us, it is extremely difficult to believe we can really believe in ourselves. It always seems easier to trust other people, to listen to someone else. Most of the time, we never realize, when we don't trust ourselves, we are prone to let little setbacks and little people take us off our mission. As soon as things get a little tough, a little tight, a little hot, we start to worry. That worry leads to negative self-talk and ultimately to self-doubt. What will it take for us to realize how powerful we are? How powerful our minds are? Sooner or later we will understand that we are our first line of defense and reference. It would be very wise to listen to yourself very carefully. You never know when you will say exactly what you need to hear.

Self-doubt damages self-worth!

EVERYBODY WANTS EVERYTHING their way, all the time. Everybody thinks everybody else is wrong most of the time. When things don't go the way we want them to go, we get mad. Then we blame somebody or anybody for not getting our way. That is what it's about: We get angry when we don't get our way. Just like children, we pout, stamp our feet, swear under our breath, and promise ourselves that one day we will have our way. Unfortunately, we didn't know how to have our way without the pain, anger, and confusion— UNTIL TODAY!

You can have your way easily and effortlessly. You can have what you want, when you want it, the way you want it, without fighting, struggling, or being pissed off. You can have as much as you want, of whatever it is, in whatever size, quantity, or style you desire. In order for this to happen, you must fulfill one tiny requirement: make the decision. Once you decide, don't waver or falter or doubt or accept anything less than what you've decided on. Don't get mad or impatient or fearful that it won't show up. Once you make the decision, trust that things will fall into place and show up at just the right time.

You can have all things the divine way.

———

SOME PEOPLE HAVE a way of bringing out the worst in us. Sometimes it is the way they talk to us. For some reason they think we don't know what they know. Sometimes it's just the way they do the things they do. It just makes you crazy! Some people just show up with their face and hair and attitude and that look that makes your skin crawl. You try to be nice. You really try to like them. Yet no matter how hard you try, they just bring out the ugly in you. The next time you are in the company of someone like this, ask yourself, "Why am I giving this person my power?" Better yet, you might want to remember that God works through people —all the time!

All people, no matter what you think about them, are an embodiment of the same divine energy in you. They may not know it. You may not see it. Sometimes they may not act divine, but actions do not change the truth. People are God's hands and feet, eyes and ears. People are God's students and God's teachers. God will test you, teach you, love you through the being of another person. Your job is to honor and respect people for the part of God they are.

The next time you are challenged by one of those nerve-wracking people, remember, God is in your face! How you respond to and treat other people is always a reflection of what you know and believe about God.

I See the God in You!

JUST WHEN YOU think you have it all figured out, something will show up to make you doubt yourself. At the precise moment you think that your troubles are over and that things are finally going your way, things will appear to turn around and head in the other direction. On the very day that you are feeling up, happy, ready to go, you will get some news that will knock the wind right out of your sails. Life is just like that, so don't take it personally.

When bad times show up in the middle of good times, just sit down, get quiet, remember the truth about who you are, and pray. All things really do work together for your good. Just because things take a curve does not mean they are not on track. The curve could very well be a part of the process! Life always brings us what we are divinely entitled to, and sometimes it will not look the way we want it to look. Sometimes we are being tested. At other times we are simply being called on to surrender, to be patient, and have lots and lots of faith.

Good comes in many shapes and forms!

DEAR SELF,
People talk about you. It gets back to you.
You strike out at them;
find things wrong with them;
tell bad things about them.
But do you really look at yourself?
Sometimes talk comes to you because you need to
hear it.
But you don't want to hear anything about your "self."
You indulge your "self" in
greatness, righteousness, aggrandizement, and
ego-gratification.
If you are so great, so wonderful, so marvelous,
why is this information coming to you?
DETACH and LISTEN!
There may be something in it you can use.

Maybe you are telling me something I need to hear.

NO MATTER WHO you are and how much you know, you are not always right. Even when you are not right, it does not mean you are wrong. It may simply mean there is something you cannot see, do not fully understand, or have not taken into consideration.

When we hold on to the need to always be right, we close ourselves off to the energy of Divine Mind which is always at work in and through other people. When we allow our "rightness" to cut others off, we limit the new information Divine Mind offers us.

Very often we look at what people do or how they look and determine we know or are more than they. In other cases, past experiences, what we know or have heard about a person entices us to judge them or their ability and knowledge. In a universe where we are all connected to the same life force, judging is not the "right" or the "righteous" thing to do. You may be right about what you feel, and still this does not make the other person wrong. They may have done a wrong thing, but this does not contribute to making you right.

Right and wrong are judgments we make in response to our own perceptions. The need to always be right or to prove your rightness to and above others is a reflection of the self-perception that somehow, somewhere you are not so right.

Today, do not need to be right.

PEOPLE CAN CALL you names, accuse you unjustly, slander you behind your back, but they cannot change who you are and the truth you know about yourself. Very often we can get so caught up in the injustice and unfairness of the actions of others, we have a temporary lapse of memory. We may say or do things which, to an uninvolved observer, give credence to the very things people are saying.

Always remember who you are. Know that you are never required to apologize to anyone for being yourself. People may not like it, but they, like you, are still growing. If you have conducted yourself honorably, with good intent, giving 100 percent of yourself and your energy to your endeavors, do not waste time defending yourself against what others may call you. The truth needs no defense. It will stand on its own in the face of any opposition and against the most powerful adversary. Be willing to make amends if you have in fact acted out of principle or spoken hastily. Be prepared to engage in self-reflection and correction. When you can do these things and act with a clear conscience, you will not be derailed by what other people call you.

Respond to the truth within yourself!

BEFORE YOUR MOTHER was your mother, she was a playful little girl who hated bugs, loved candy, and never wanted to go to bed when she was sent. She was an adolescent with zits and no breasts who wanted a boyfriend. She was a teenager who had cramps and who wanted a prom date to kiss her in the places her momma said were off-limits. She was a young woman ready to leave home but afraid to go. She had problems and fears and bad days.

Before your mother was your mother, she had dreams, she had goals, and, yes, she had a life. Then she had you. Even if she didn't expect you, she welcomed you. She gave you the best of who she was and what she had, even when it didn't look like it. She was afraid for herself and even more so for you, even if she never said anything about it. She wanted you to have things that she didn't have to give you. She wanted to tell you things she couldn't bring herself to say. There were times she hurt your feelings. At other times she made you mad. In the middle of your struggles with her, you probably never considered everything your mother was before she was your mother; she still is and will be forever.

Mothers are people too.

WHEN YOU ARE so sure that someone is out to hurt you, it becomes very difficult to forgive their shortcomings. It is much easier to believe that people develop clever and malicious ways to inflict wounds on you than it is to accept that they are merely human, doing what humans do. For some strange reason, it is much easier to take everything very personally rather than to accept people as they are, forgive them for what they do, and release them from our lives. We know very well how to be a victim. Being a person who refuses to be victimized seems to be where we have trouble.

Perhaps it is easier to be a victim, because if we really try to understand people we will see many pieces of our self. If we see those pieces of our self, we would have to forgive other people. Forgiveness takes courage. Courage begins in character. A good solid character requires a level of self-esteem so many of us believe we do not have. One way you can enhance your self-esteem is to stop being so willing to be a victim. In order not to be a victim, we must develop the courage to speak up for ourselves. The only way we can develop this kind of courage is to be real clear about who we are. When we know who we are, we will realize that no one can do anything to harm us unless we keep them around and allow them to do so.

Be as willing to stand up as you are to bow down.

YOUR CHILDREN'S FAILURES are not your failures, and you can't kill the kids when they mess up. For some reason, mothers believe everything the children do is a reflection on their motherhood. A mother can be totally devoted, always present, giving her best, and have a child go totally astray. Children make choices. Children make decisions. Children can and do mess up. When they do, no amount of yelling, threats, and motherly guilt will change what has happened. The best you can do is support and assist them in working through whatever it is.

Our children come "through" us into life to learn their lessons and have the experiences they need in order to find their true identity. Whatever we do, and however we do it, is the best we have to offer. Our job is to guide, support, nurture, teach, and lay the foundation for them to stand on. Sometimes we miss the mark. Sometimes we get caught up in our own lessons and experiences. Sometimes we give the best of what we have and who we are, and they still fail. It's all okay. Know that the same God who watches you watches your children. Also know, no matter what, your children are equipped to fall, get up, and fall again. If or when they do, your job is to breathe! Pray! And Have Faith!

Do your best. Give your best. Expect the best from the children.

HAVE YOU EVER been in an airplane when it is changing directions? Usually there is a drop in altitude. There may even be some turbulence which will cause your stomach to flip and your heart to flutter. There is a loss of speed. Or the plane may pick up speed and then drop, suddenly and unexpectedly, which can be very frightening. Changing directions in life is like hitting turbulence in the air, and fear is the normal response to the turbulence caused by change. Things are going to be rough for a while, but you must hold on and ride it out.

When the turbulence of change hits you, make believe you are a pilot, well trained and experienced, able to ride out the turbulence until a tailwind takes you up again. If that doesn't work, make believe you are a stewardess. Keep yourself calm, give yourself encouragement, stand firmly and confidently that all is well, no matter how rough it gets. If you are afraid of flying, just lay down on the floor, cover your head, and don't worry about the turbulence. In any case, always remember that God is your landing strip, able to handle your weight, ready to receive you; even if you fall, you will still be on solid ground!

Hold on for a change!

———

ON YOUR JOURNEY to do better, you are going to find obstacles. The obstacles in your path are there to make you stronger. Building a new life is hard work, and you will need muscles. Obstacles build muscles—big, strong muscles which you can flex.

On the path to empowerment you are going to be challenged. Challenges make you quick on your feet. They teach you how to bob and weave. Moving into your power is going to make people nervous. They are going to challenge your new ideas, your new approach, and the new you that is emerging. Challenges make you think and rethink what you are doing. Thinking strengthens the mind. The strong mind of a powerful person has nothing to fear when challenged. A strong mind can weave together an answer for the people who challenge it—GET A LIFE! is a good place to start.

On your climb to the top, people are going to throw stones at you. Don't worry about it; you are strong, you can bob, weave, and get out of the way. The stones they throw may be very big, and they will come at you from the most unlikely places, at the most inopportune moments. Don't stop climbing! Don't look back! Stay focused! The people who are throwing stones will be so intent on hitting you they may not realize that the stones they are throwing up at you are going to come back down and hit them on the head.

I can take it! I can make it!

THINK ABOUT ALL that God is. God is peace, joy, strength, power, abundance, truth, and love. God is not pain, anger, fear, confusion, restriction, or destruction. So often we find ourselves in painful, frightening, and destructive situations that limit our freedom or make us unhappy. For some reason we convince ourselves that where we are is where God wants us to be. If it is not peace, joy, love, and harmony, it is not God!

God does not want us to be in pain. However, God will not interfere with the choices we make. If we choose to stay in an abusive relationship, an unfulfilling job, a chaotic family environment, or any other harmful situation, God will not interfere! God cannot move us until we are ready to be moved. God cannot help us until we are ready to be helped. God cannot save us unless we want to be saved. When we understand who God really is and how that relates to who we are, we are free to choose a better way of living. When we choose better God moves in mysterious ways!

Today, choose God!

The Valley of Courage

*Teaches us to surrender our fears and secret
thoughts about ourselves and the world by
developing trust in the universe of life.*

*S*ee the inevitable changes not as threats
but as opportunities that can deepen
our understanding and bring us wisdom
and growth.

—SUSAN L. TAYLOR

DEAR SELF,
In the right moment, in the perfect way;
I will be shown what to do.
I will be told what to say.
Until then, I will love myself,
I will honor myself,
and I will be still.

I will be shown the divine way.

THERE IS A little girl inside of you who never grew up. She has been there from the beginning. She has seen, heard, experienced every aspect of your life. She knows, she really knows who you are; and she never misses an opportunity to remind you. She knows your strengths, weaknesses, fears, likes, and dislikes. She knows who you are, what you can do; most of all, she knows when and how to act up.

Children will act up at the most inconvenient times. They will lose things. They will spill things on their clothes. They will make you late. They will speak out at inappropriate times. They have temper tantrums. They overeat. They fight, argue, and take things that do not belong to them. All to get your attention.

Don't ignore your little girl. Make sure you greet her, nurture her, talk to her, every day. Find ways to reassure her, make her feel safe. Let her know she is loved, welcomed, valued. Let her play, and make sure she has plenty of toys. Don't forget to discipline her. Be firm but supportive, structured but flexible. Encourage her to try new things. Listen to her opinions. Make sure she eats well and gets plenty of rest. You may be all grown up. However, there is a little girl in you still trying to figure out who she is and what life is really about.

Honor the child in you!

WHEN THE THING that we really want finally does show up in our lives, we usually have two emotions at the same time, joy and terror! We can be so excited that we are finally getting what we want that we are terrorized by what it means. It means that life really is on our side. It means that we really do deserve to have what we want. It also means that our hard work is paying off and that things are getting ready to change . . . drastically.

The conflicting emotions of joy and terror send a message of urgency through our body that sometimes kills off our joy. We can become so engrossed in the terror of losing, of moving, and of changing that we lose sight of the answered prayer. Terror makes you busy. Busyness can lead to self-sabotage! When you find yourself in a state of urgency, check in with yourself to make sure that you are not allowing terror to steal your joy.

Do not terrorize yourself!

✳ IT IS POSSIBLE to know the truth and not tell the truth. The line between knowledge of truth and the ability to tell it is called discipline. Truth without discipline is like wearing lead-bottom shoes. You know what to do or say, yet you cannot move to do it. The weight of the knowledge holds you down. You want to move this knowledge or information off your back, but to keep a friend, keep the peace, stay within your comfort zone, you excuse yourself from responsibility. Now you are weighed down with self-doubt, self-criticism, and self-denial.

Truth supported by discipline is like a hot knife on butter. With it you can cut through fear, doubt, and the annoying habits which erode your discipline and cast shadows on the truth. If you really want to grow spiritually, you must discipline your mind to seek truth, your mouth to speak the truth, and yourself to live in truth. Only then will your heart be opened to know the truth of God.

Truth is my first line of defense.

SO MANY OF us are afraid to die, we fail to live. We will not take chances when they present any form of risk. They are too dangerous. Danger can lead to death. We may be afraid to drive, afraid to fly. Too afraid to say yes. Even more afraid to say no. We are afraid to be alone. Even more afraid to go out. When we don't live because of the fear of dying, we die without ever having lived.

What part of life are you missing when you live in fear of dying? Are you not already dead to those experiences? You may convince yourself you can live without them, but are you really living? Are you really alive when you tuck yourself away from people or experiences you believe can hurt you, harm you, or in some way take your life away? There is a way to escape the fear of death. Consider the fact that you started dying the moment you were born.

Today, I am going to live all of life.

Dreaming can be frightening.
When you dream,
all things are possible.
I like to dream.
But it can be frightening to imagine that you can have
anything, everything that you want.
It's mind-blowing to imagine that there is a place
where all your needs are met,
where all of your wishes can come true;
that you can live the type of life
you have dreamed of without struggle or effort.
Can you imagine doing all of the things you love to do;
being paid for doing those things;
feeling good about what you are doing and yourself.
Is that frightening to you?
It's frightening to me!
That is probably why it is not happening!
I am afraid to dream.

No dream is too good to come true.

*God is there because I am here.
I am here because God is there.*

There is a very subtle difference between these two statements which can make a world of difference in the way we approach life. When we understand that we are God's eyes, ears, hands, and feet we can have a little more confidence in ourselves. From on high, God is dependent on us to demonstrate His/Her work. It's on us to give love, bring peace, demonstrate power, utilize compassion, be forgiving, show mercy, and live in grace. That is what God does up there.

When we believe the only reason we are here is because God put us here, the journey becomes overwhelming. We feel unclear and unfocused. We believe we are limited and powerless. We wait around for special instructions because we believe we have to be special. No one can tell us what to do. We are the bosses. It is your job here on earth to remind people that we all have the power to create a good life, a better life. It's not God's job to make life better for us. God sent us here to make life better.

God is present and accountable for me.

STAND UP! YOU have the power of Queens in your blood. The sacredness of the eagles in your bones. The fierceness of warriors in your genes. The wisdom of the grandmothers is in the recesses of your mind, accessible to you through the energy of spirit.

STAND UP! Take the responsibility for defining yourself and determining your own destiny. Believe you have the power. Understand who you are. Don't be so willing to take someone else's word about what is best for you.

STAND UP! Celebrate the wisdom of life in your spirit. Dare to do, to be, to reach and stretch beyond the boundaries of humanness to the unlimited world of spirit. The universe will back you up. The Father will hold you up. The Mother will keep you up. That means you have Holy Boldness! STAND UP and show it off.

I stand in Holy Boldness!

THE NATION, THE community, the family are all one race of people—Human! Our spirit is a holistic spirit. In our hearts and minds and from our mouths, we must begin to promote the good of the whole. One man on drugs affects the whole. One homeless woman affects the whole. One hungry child affects the whole. When we ignore what affects the whole, it weakens the nation. It undermines the community. It breaks the family ties. It destroys the spirit.

I have something to offer the whole.

I can't tell anybody about this.

SOMETIMES KEEPING THINGS inside makes them seem worse than they are. There's so much going on inside: the past, the future, the present, not to mention normal bodily functions. The weight of it all is tearing you up, holding you down; it may feel like you want to burst. If you don't talk about it, you will.

The Value in the Valley states, "A wound needs air in order to heal." There comes a time when it becomes necessary to open ourselves up for review and examination by talking about our pain. It's not easy. As a matter of fact, it's frightening. We don't want to expose ourselves to public speculation or criticism. We don't want to admit our frailties or follies. Goodness knows, we don't want to face the pain, fear, anger, shame, or guilt attached to our deepest thoughts and feelings. Yet when what is going on inside hinders what we are able to do, we must talk about it.

Find somebody you can trust. Find someone you don't know and may never see again. Call a help line, hot line, or prayer line. Find someone you can talk to about what you feel. You are not looking for an answer or a resolution; you are in search of a release. If you can't find a living person, go into a quiet place and talk to God.

I've got to talk about it.

YOU MUST KNOW at all times, in all situations, under every possible circumstance, you can depend on God. God, the good, powerful essence of life is always within you, always around you, always holding and lifting you up. The very essence and energy of God is actually what you are. Yet in times of difficulty, we forget this. For some of us, we never knew it in the first place.

You may have convinced yourself that you have done too much wrong for God to still be with you. This is simply not so. Perhaps the events of your life have led you to believe that God does not have the power to help you. Nothing could be further from the truth. Very often we blame God for what has happened to us. We get angry with God because things do not go the way we want them to go. In the end, we mentally and emotionally abandon God by resigning ourselves to pain and suffering! No matter what has happened, where we have been, or what we have done, we will not, cannot move beyond pain, fear, and disappointment until we realize in the deepest part of the soul, "I can depend on God."

God is the spirit of life. Life is not merely what we live, it is what we are. Even when we believe God cannot or will not help us, there is a ray of hope: God can and will help us. God will maintain and sustain the energy of life that we are.

I can depend on the life of God in me.

YOU DO WHAT you think is right, only to find out it is the worst thing you could have done. Somebody is mad at you. You're out a lot of money. You feel real bad, and you still have a big mess to clean up. Here's something you might want to remember: even when it doesn't look good, be conscious of God in every little thing you do.

God really is everywhere, all the time. God is always healing and teaching and loving us. Things may look pretty bleak right now. You might feel bad or foolish, but you never know how the Creator is going to show up or stand up. It may not be fancy or flashy. It may look confusing or frightening. You may be stressed or angry or teetering on the edge of disaster; just remember, God is in everything, everywhere, all the time.

God is always on time and in time.

DEAR SELF,
If I had to do it all over again,
I wouldn't change
what I did.
I would change
the way I felt about what I did.

What I do cannot change who I am.

NO STORM CAN last forever! It will never rain 365 days consecutively. The rain may ruin your wedding or your roof. The rain can blind you and flood out the basement. But no matter how hard it rains, one day the water will dry up. Even snow cannot fall forty, fifty, sixty days in a row. It may fall very heavy today and tomorrow. It may freeze up, creating very dangerous conditions. Just keep in mind, all the snow piled up outside your door must melt one day.

Trouble comes to pass, not to stay! Just as in a storm, you may be having a miserable time in life. Perhaps you can't get around some problem. Something or someone may have caused an incredible amount of damage to your heart, your mind, your total state of being. You may be snowed in, bogged down, flooded out by fear, anger, or emotional destruction. Don't worry! No storm, not even the one in your life, can last forever.

This storm is just passing over!

DON'T BEAT UP on yourself if you did not make it through the diet. If you cannot convince yourself that you can make it without a cigarette, a candy bar, that extra piece of chicken, or just one bag of potato chips, it's okay. Even if you hate the job and know you should leave, or love the man and know it's not going to work, try not to be so hard on yourself for staying. Whatever you are doing that you know you must stop doing, you cannot stop doing it until you are ready.

Talking ready is not enough. Thinking ready will not work. You must "be" ready in mind, body, and spirit before you can make a change. All of your circuits must be positioned on "go." Until then, people cannot convince you to do it. You cannot force you to do it. No book or song or magic potion can make you move before you are ready. Everything you think, say, and do until that happens is just preparation. So love yourself right now. Honor yourself anyway. Keep talking to yourself. Keep thinking ready thoughts. In the meantime, try to remember you will not be ready until you are ready.

Ready is as ready does!

COURAGE NOT ONLY means being able to do something new. It also means taking steps to "be" someone new. Some of us talk a great deal because we are afraid we won't be heard. Others never say anything in fear of saying the wrong thing. Some of us are overactive and hyperactive because we fear missing out. There are those of us who are withdrawn, lethargic, inactive, in fear of messing up.

One of the first steps in developing a courageous outlook and approach to life is being able to look at ourselves, our beliefs, attitudes, and patterns. Courage enables us to examine. Examination enables us to choose. Courage is more than forceful, aggressive, bold outward action. At its most infinite level, courage is an in-depth, inward examination which leads to alteration and application of a new way to be.

Courage creates a new state of being!

SO YOU THINK you are not good enough, not "God" enough. You've been doing everything you should, the way you should, and still the changes, if any, are slow in coming, almost insignificant. You keep wondering what more can you do, how much more should you know, to get yourself, your life, to the point of peace and plenty you desire. You're asking when will it get better? When will you be better? Maybe, just maybe, things are the way they need to be. That doesn't mean things will not get better. It means they take time.

Every seed planted takes time to grow. Every thought that crosses your mind is a seed. Every word you speak is a seed. Every action you take is a seed in the garden of life. You cannot see how the seed germinates. You will not see the roots sprout and take hold in the deep darkness of the earth. Unless you watch very carefully, you will not see that first little stalk poke its head up through the earth. If you move too quickly, you will trample the first leaves of the tiny plant.

Doubt, worry, anxiety will retard the growth of spiritual seeds. You are a sprout in God's garden. Your roots are growing stronger and taking hold with every ounce of faith and trust you pour forth. God is a good gardener. S/He showers love and mercy and grace on the garden of life every day. God's seeds may grow slowly, but as long as God has anything to do with it, they grow strong in divine time and order.

All seeds take time to grow.

I'VE GOT ASTHMA! I don't have the money!
I'm not smart enough! It's too hard! I'm too old!
I've got kids! He won't let me! It is very easy to
find reasons not to do the things we say we want to do.
Once we convince ourselves that we have a good enough
excuse, we have a reason to be unhappy, stuck, unproductive.

Physical, financial, and emotional challenges are real.
They create boundaries in our lives. However, no one said
we cannot move beyond boundaries. Your life is a reflection of what you believe. If you really believe something
or someone can stop you, it can, and . . . it will! But you
already know that. What you may not know is that what
you tell yourself about yourself, about your life, about
your limitations, you will believe. What you believe is the
foundation of what you do and don't do.

There is nothing so wrong that it cannot be made
right. There is nothing so heavy that it can't be lifted.
There is nothing so bad, so ugly, so horrible, so heavy, so
deep, that you can't work through it, move around it, step
over it, but you have to believe it. If you don't believe it,
you can't do it.

You can! Yes! You can!

YOU MAY NOT own your home, a car, or a fine array of clothes. You may not have stocks, securities, or an impressive amount of cash. You may work for someone you have never seen, depend on people you don't know to provide food for your table, and pay taxes to an institution that has relegated you to an identifiable number. Still, you own something that is more valuable than any of these things. What you own is your mind, and your mind produces very valuable thoughts.

Every thought you have is your personal property, to do with as you choose. Like everything else you own, your thoughts are precious. When you understand just how valuable thoughts are, perhaps you will own your home. Maybe that car you want will be yours. You may continue working for someone and paying taxes to someone else, but owning your thoughts will give you a completely different perspective. When you own your thoughts and value them, it means you realize that they are powerful enough to create any experience you want.

A thought is a valuable possession.

DEAR SELF,
When you panic, you do things in fear.
The moment you think the thoughts;
speak the words;
commit the acts;
you know you are out of balance and out of control.
Yet for some reason,
you cannot stop yourself.
When it is over, you go into remorse;
beating yourself, feeling bad, being sorry.
It is important to learn to stop yourself
at the panic stage.
When you sense the fear, panic, desperation welling up
in your heart and mind,
you must get still and say,
"STOP!"
"I will not panic!"
"I will not go into fear!"
I Will Be Still!

Please! Don't panic!

At the sound of the tone,
leave your name and your need;
God and Goodness
will make sure you get exactly
what you ask for.

Before I ask, God knows my needs!

The Valley of Knowledge and Wisdom

Teaches us to develop the courage, strength,
obedience, and discipline
to act on what we know to be true.

*T*here's an old saying: only little children
and old folks tell the truth.
When you get real old, you just
lay it on the table.

—BESSIE DELANY

DEAR GOD,

Please order my thoughts today. Place in my mind those things that are a priority to you. Those things that will establish divine order in this life you have given me. Take away the thoughts, habits, attitudes which create fear and keep me from being in alignment with Your will. Help me to see things through Your eyes, according to Your law. Take away every thought, want, unconscious and conscious urge that can place me on the treadmill of pain and confusion. Fill my mind with Your will, Your way, Your desire for me today. Help me to see all things from a divine perspective today, a perspective of love, peace, and joy. And then, Lord, guide me to act accordingly. Thank You, God.

Today, my thoughts are ordered.

You CANNOT COME to God with your hands full. You cannot expect spirit to lift you up if you come with clenched fist. Very often we seek the assistance, support, guidance of the Most High when we are filled to the brim with our own "stuff." We come with preconceived notions; fixed ideas and opinions; judgments and criticisms of others, very structured demands of what we need, how we want it, and what we are willing to do or not do to get it. The universe cannot work that way!

If everyone got what they wanted, exactly the way they wanted it, there would be no room for divine intervention or improvement. What about the demands we make when we are angry, frightened, upset, or desperate? Very often the things we cry out for in the moment are not things we really want or need. And let us not forget those occasions when we asked for help while hiding something behind our backs. Something we didn't want anyone else to know; something we were ashamed to admit; something hidden in the subconscious mind. We may not have remembered, realized, or understood what it was, but the universe did and responded accordingly.

No matter how afraid, ashamed, angry, or upset we may be, we must empty out before we face the divine. The best way to get what you need, just in the nick of time, is to come to God with nothing in hand.

I come with open hands.

EVERYTHING IN LIFE is a process. Events occur one at a time until the process is complete. When you are faced with a difficulty in life, the question you must first answer is, what is my process? What are the steps I can take to begin working through and out of this situation? If you are an average, warm-blooded human being, you probably don't have a process. Like the rest of us, the process is to panic. Until today!

No matter what is going on, you can only do one thing at a time. If you panic, you can't think. First step, think. Make every effort to have a bite-size idea of what is happening. Ten words or less should be just fine. Look at one issue or problem at a time. Next, take yourself out of the situation. Depersonalize and defuse the situation by allowing yourself to become the third party. Think in terms of, look what is happening to her/him. Third step, examine everything you know about what is going on: who is involved, what has happened, what needs to happen. Resist blaming or imagining the worst, being angry or afraid. This is not about you; you are an observer.

Final step, without looking to outside forces, honestly place responsibility where it should be, with the resources and information available right now; advise the person how to proceed. Don't worry about what might happen. Don't take the path of least resistance. Do what is honest, just, peaceful, and in the best interest of all. After you tell the other person how to proceed, do it!

Let me get out of the way of the process!

HOW ARE YOU going to handle it this time? You have probably been here before, in this or a similar situation. You undoubtedly learned something, even if you didn't fully understand or like the lesson. Well, here you are again! The issue is, how are you going to handle it this time? What are you going to do? How will you choose to respond?

As we travel through life, the scenery changes, the players come and go, but the truth remains constant. Our lessons are consistent. Our experiences are testing tools by which life examines us and gives us the opportunity to examine ourselves. As we progress, life knows what we know, even when we think we don't know. How are you going to respond? What are you going to do this time? Are you going to pout, stamp your feet, put your hands on your hips, and create drama? Or are you going to practice what you know, follow your heart, honor yourself, and grow? The choice is yours, but remember, life is watching you. Don't fail the test!

I am willing to do a new thing.

THERE ARE MANY ways to learn your lessons and receive your good in life. Only you can determine how you will do it. Some of us get it quick! We get in a little bit of trouble or experience a little bit of pain. It will cause us to drop to one knee to pray for mercy. We get the point and move on, never to repeat that lesson again. For some of us, it takes a little longer. We will persist in doing things our way until the pain, the confusion, or the stress become so intense, we must drop to two knees to beg and plead for mercy before we get the point. Then, there are those of us who do not get the point, and are not even aware that a point exists until we are flat on our face in the mud! We are what my grandmother called "hard-headed."

When you see that things are not working out, don't insist that they do! Back up! Detach! Take some time to assess the situation. Always remember, your blessings have your name on them. No one can take them away from you. There is no need to rush, push, stress yourself out to get to your good. It will come to you at the divine time in the divine way. The condition you are in when the blessing shows up is totally up to you—on one knee, on two knees, or with your face full of mud!

When you get it, you will get it!

THE TRUTH OF the matter is, you will not always know what to do. Unfortunately, you may not know that you don't know, until you know. That can be dangerous. When you don't know that you don't know, you run around trying to convince others that you know. If they don't know that you don't know they will follow you, because they think you know. But we know that won't work because you really don't know. And if they know, but think they don't know, that you don't know, nobody knows whether or not you know what they think they don't know. Do you see how confusing it can be?

You can save yourself a great deal of trouble by admitting to yourself and them, I'm not sure I know. Actually, you do know, but you must be still in order to come to that realization. In stillness, you will know that you know, and that's all you need to know in order to move forward.

I know I'm not confused!

IF YOU DRIVE too fast, you might miss your turn. If you walk too fast, you might pass where you are going. If you speak too quickly, you demonstrate that you have missed the point. Slow down! You cannot arrive at your destination until you get there. Along the way, take in the scenery. Stop, sit a spell, and rest yourself. There's a lot going on in life and in you. If you zip around, you are bound to miss something. If and when you do, resist the urge to blame other people. Tell the truth! You know you were moving, talking, wanting too much, too fast.

Slowly I move, step by step!

DO WE YELL at children when they fall down and bump their heads or bust their lips? No. Do we punch guests who break glasses or spill drinks? No. Do we lash out at plants that die or flowers that don't bloom? No. Somehow we find compassion in our hearts to forgive and excuse the mishaps and errors of others. Yet we have little if any compassion for ourselves. For some reason, we tend to forget we are growing and learning, and that we will fall down and sometimes make a mess.

You may not always know what to do. It's okay! You will not always be able to find the right words at the moment you need them. It's okay! You may swear you won't and then do it anyway. It really is okay! It's okay if you do, or say, or forget to do or say the "right" thing at the "right" time. The challenge is to learn not to beat yourself up about it.

It's okay because I'm okay.

WHEN CHAOS, CONFUSION, difficulty show up in our lives, we must go back to the beginning. Not to the beginning of the problem, but the beginning of life; before life got messed up, got to be hard, got to be more than we could handle. We must go back to the beginning, before we got in trouble, got fired, got our hearts broken. We probably don't remember that time because we were in the womb. We were innocent, defenseless, helpless children of God. And, whether we realize it or not, we haven't changed a bit.

God is like the womb around us, squeezing, pushing, prodding us through the circumstances of life. Remember, the beginning of the birth process is painful. We are in darkness; we can't see. We are frightened; we do not know what to do. We want the pressure, pain, pushing to be over . . . Now!

But life doesn't happen like that. In the beginning of a new life, the womb must contract to strengthen our muscles and push us into alignment. The safe and familiar environment in which we have existed becomes chaotic; it becomes uncomfortable. In the beginning, we called it labor. Now it feels like confusion. We must remember, there comes a time when the womb pushes us forward from the old to the new. It may not feel good, but in the beginning God was there with us, around us and in us. When we remember the beginning, we realize that in just a little while, we will have a bundle of joy in our midst.

It is not confusion, it's birth.

YOU MUST TELL the truth! The whole truth, if you want to be helped out of a bad situation. So often we run to people, asking for their help or assistance, but we don't tell them the whole story. We leave out the pieces that could make us look bad. We skip over the parts we think will make them think we are stupid. More often than not, we conveniently forget to mention what we did that got us into the situation in the first place.

People cannot help you if you do not give them all the facts, all pertinent pieces of information. The truth is complete. It is whole. It is real. The truth, no matter how bad you think it sounds! The truth, even when it makes you look bad or foolish! The truth! No matter what you think the other person needs to hear in order to get them to help you! The truth, and nothing but the truth, will get you to the support, the help, the freedom you desire. If you only give half of the truth, you can only receive half of the solution!

What I'm about to say is the absolute truth!

WE DON'T GET in trouble because of what we do. We get in trouble when we do it in spite of reliable warnings and cautions, against all good advice, and in defiance of good common sense. All of us have things that we are obsessive about. We insist and push, or scheme and connive to make sure this thing will happen. Sometimes we do it to prove we are right or to prove someone else is wrong. We may do it when we are angry or afraid. Or we may do it just to prove we can do it.

We may know the behavior is unproductive or inappropriate. We may know it is foolish or dangerous. Still we insist it must be done. That is how we get ourselves in trouble or hurt or embarrassed. In response to what we do, we feel bad, beat up on ourselves, or blame others for making us or letting us do it. Whatever we do, we do it because we need to do it. No matter how foolish, hazardous, or outlandish it may be, it is simply another lesson we must learn in the classroom of life.

This is something I must do to learn my lesson!

HOW DO YOU know whom to trust? When you are in a bad situation, people may offer you help or advice, but you have been led astray before. You have been hurt and lied to before. How are you supposed to know who is real and who is not real? People say things that you want to believe, but something in your gut sets off bells and whistles in your head! How are you supposed to know what to do? Is it you? Is it them? Whom do you trust?

Each of us has been faced with the dilemma of not knowing what to do and whom to trust. The easiest way to solve the dilemma is to ask yourself, "Can I be trusted?" "Have I told the truth in this situation?" "Have I honored my word?" If you have, chances are those who are coming forward to help you can and will. If you have not, you are the issue, not the other person. You are harboring old memories, old guilt, old shame. The way to resolve the issue is to confess your errors to yourself, forgive yourself, and come clean with everyone else. Until your heart and mind are cleansed, you cannot make a decision to trust others because you know you cannot trust yourself.

When you live the truth, tell the truth, and release the past, you have no reason not to trust *them* or yourself.

Trust yourself to know the truth when you see it!

DEAR SELF,
Free your mind from the dead things
you wanted to do but allowed yourself to believe
you weren't good enough, smart enough, young or old
enough to do.
Free your heart from the fear that someone
can stop you or harm you.
Free your self from self-imposed limitations
of age, color, and gender.
Free your body from the harmful things you love
even when you know they are
absolutely no good for you.
Freedom is the key.
You must not let anything or anyone
confine or define you!

Freedom is a state of mind.

WHEN I THOUGHT I was fat, I could not find anything nice that fit my size. When I told myself I was ugly, people treated me in ugly ways.

In the book *Practicing the Presence,* Joel Goldsmith reminds us, "Every issue we face in life grows out of and stems from the well of our consciousness." Many of us do not realize that whatever we experience in our day-to-day lives and relationships is a mirror reflection of the deepest belief we hold about our self. Whether we are fired, jilted, or defamed, insulted or blamed, there is something that goes on in our consciousness that has attracted us to every experience we have.

Take a moment right now and ask yourself, when was the last time I complimented me? Have I told myself that I love me lately? How often do I criticize myself? Beat up on myself in thought, word, and deed? *You Are Always Your Own Experience.* It is a bitter pill to swallow. A challenging concept to examine. Just for today, pay close attention to how you think about you; what you say to you; how you behave toward you. If you do not like what is going on in your life, you may want to adjust your attitude about you.

What I think about me, I Am.

IT IS DANGEROUS, spiritually dangerous, to believe that everyone is wrong and you are right.

Granted, there are times when you go into a situation with the best of intentions, when you work hard, give your all, and things do not turn out the way you expected them to turn out. It is even possible for it to appear that people are against you, out to get you, doing their best to do you in. However, it is dangerous, spiritually dangerous, for you to believe that everybody else is wrong and you are right.

Always remember, the most difficult adversary and the biggest obstacle can teach you a powerful lesson. When we take up arms in opposition to people and conditions, we run the risk of missing the lesson. If we judge people by their behavior, criticize them because of their different opinion and approach, it is easy to become self-righteous. We can easily identify what we do that is correct in the face of others we deem incorrect. What is not always so easy to see is how challenging people and situations can strengthen us. We become frustrated, often angry, when we cannot get people to see our way or to be the way we believe they should be. In the process, we miss the opportunity to be patient, tolerant, or cooperative. In the most challenging situations, we overlook a golden opportunity to see a new way, do a new thing. That can be most dangerous and damaging to the spirit.

Every point is a good point!

SOME OF US are born into dark circumstances. As children we grow up in the midst of dark experiences. In response, we may think dark thoughts and come to the conclusion that darkness is all we can expect. In the midst of darkness we are limited as to what we can see. We see and expect very little for ourselves because the world of darkness has little to offer. It has taken all the light from our dreams.

The story of Jabez in the Bible speaks to the issue of darkness. Jabez, like so many of us, had very little to look forward to in life. What Jabez held onto, which many of us lose in the darkness, is character. Jabez's character remained strong through his faith. He kept that faith active with prayer. In prayer, Jabez did not limit his expectations to what he could see; he asked for all the goodness, grace, and favor that God had to offer in order to make him strong enough to move out of his dark circumstances into the light of Spirit.

We must remember to be like Jabez, faithful, prayerful, strong in the spirit of our character. When we find ourselves in the shadows of darkness, we must not limit ourselves to only what we can see in the glow of a 40-watt bulb! We must pray for what we know is present under the glow of 100 watts.

Darkness must give way to the light!

WHEN DIFFICULTY OR trouble shows up in your life, the first instinct is to tighten up. Your body becomes tense. Your mind closes in on the situation at hand. You may shut your eyes, grit your teeth, and clench your fists. Your tightness is probably intensified when the situation has something to do with money. Money trouble causes a restriction in the brain. You want to pinch pennies, stretch dollars, and hold on to what you have.

Tightening up or holding on in the time of trouble, particularly financial trouble, is the worst thing you can do! You are holding onto the trouble. You are demonstrating your belief in lack. When you tighten up, you restrict your thoughts, and that may keep your good from coming in. You tighten the grip of energy around the very thing you don't want—lack! The best way, actually the only way, to get out of trouble is to give your lack a way out!

Giving activates the law of correspondence; what you give must come back to you tenfold. Giving is an act of faith. It is the only way that you can demonstrate your belief in the abundance of life, the goodness of God, and the wealth that is yours by divine right. And the best time to give is when you think you don't have enough to give. Give your time, your energy, your knowledge, your resources, and your money. Giving is a blessing, and you can never out-bless God!

Give what you have. Get what you need!

PSALM 37 IS one of my favorite passages in the Bible. "Fret not thyself because of evil doers."

We must keep this passage in mind when we see people receiving good that we may believe they do not deserve. At times it may seem that while we are doing all the work and getting nowhere, others come along, do very little, and are rewarded greatly. The truth is, we really don't know what they have done or what they deserve. Most of the time, we judge based on appearances and experience, which may or may not tell the entire story.

Then there are those times when we know that people are unethical, unprincipled, or dishonest. It may appear to us that they are getting away with it. We become upset and sometimes angry with them and with ourselves. We may question our worth and our methods. We may even question the wisdom of God. The truth is, no one gets away with anything they do in life. A few ill-gotten gains will quickly fall away when the hand of universal justice passes over. You can only have what is rightfully yours. You make the choice about how you will receive it: righteously and permanently or wrongfully and temporarily!

You get what is rightfully yours righteously.

THE ENERGY AND work required for spiritual growth and transformation offer very few short-term rewards. The work is hard, and the hours are long. There will be times when it seems as if you are getting nowhere—real fast! It will appear to you that others are passing you by and still others are gaining on you. Some will even appear to step over you or on you. You will get tired. You will get discouraged. You will want to give up . . . but you won't!

Most of us are conditioned to expect short-term rewards for the things we do in life. Study hard, get an A. Work hard, get paid. Look good, get complimented. Spiritual growth does not work like that! You must work hard and exercise what you know before you reap the benefits of what you know. And the more you know, the harder you must work to exercise the principles in all situations and under all circumstances. In the process of all of this work, no one is going to be grading you. You may never get a compliment. Your bank account may not reflect how hard you have worked or how much you know. But in the end, you will have such peace of mind and inner strength, those things won't matter to you anyway.

Spiritual work brings long-term rewards.

DEAR SELF,

Let me remember:
The Father and I are one!
God's plan for me is my salvation!
There is nothing I want that I cannot have!
I must be willing to forgive!
I make the choice about who I am and who I become!
The time is now!
What I can't do, God can do!
I am my sister!
Right where I am, the light of God, the power of God,
the peace of God,
and the love of God are too!
I must always be grateful!

Love,
God's gift to me!

God always works on your behalf!

THE MINUTE JEAN heard there was something wrong with somebody, she had to rescue them. She was a fixer who usually felt broken. Carol always had an excuse for doing or not doing something in a particular way. The way she did things usually left her feeling used up, drained, and unappreciated. Mae was a blamer. It was never her fault. Someone had done it to her or made her do it this time and that time. Joan didn't do anything unpleasant. She either ate, drank, or went to sleep. These women were totally unaware of what they were doing to contribute to their undoing. They did it habitually, believing they couldn't help it.

There is a price we must all pay to feel good in life. That price is attention. We must pay attention to what we do and what we get in return. We must pay attention to how we feel before, during, and after we do our thing. When we find that what we are doing does not make us feel good or empowered, we must stop doing it. We must not let fear for others or ourselves, excuses, or mindless meanderings repeatedly prompt us to take unproductive actions. Pay attention. Attention must be paid. If you do not watchfully attend to what you do, you will find yourself where you don't want to be . . . again.

I am attending to my goodness.

THERE ARE TIMES when you want to make a mark on the world. You may want to make a statement. You may want to make a name for yourself. You may believe that the best way to make this happen is to take a big project and refuse to let people support, assist, or help you. You want to do it all because you have something to prove. Beneath that rationale is the truth that you want to get all the credit. There is nothing wrong with having a desire to be recognized and rewarded. What you probably don't want is the confusion and stress being in charge and in control can cause you.

The mark of a good leader is the ability to delegate and share responsibility. A good leader knows how to allow other people to do the work. A true leader is surrounded by good people who share the vision and do the work because they believe in what they are doing. Your job is to find these people and hire them. A leader can step out of the way, let the workers work, and know in the end, the leader gets the credit. What a good leader does when she gets the credit is give it away. A true leader is humble and willing to serve because a leader knows the best way to make a name for yourself is to create it within yourself. The world already knows that a good leader stands behind, not on top of those who do the work.

The work is a credit to the leader.

YOUR MOUTH IS the stable of your power. Every word that comes out of your mouth is like a horse. Some horses are well trained, well groomed, and well kept. These are the race horses. They have a strong and powerful energy, supported by their ability. When a race horse leaves the stable, it is expected that the horse will bring the owner many rewards.

Other horses are wild stallions that buck and kick. Once they are out of the stable, it is hard to catch them. It is even harder to get them back into the stable. A wild stallion can be destructive. It can run down, run over, even kill something. A stallion on the loose, which cannot be caught or brought back to the stable, will usually cause harm or bring disgrace to the owner.

Nags are kept in a stable too. These slow-moving beasts are almost useless and serve no good purpose. Nags just hang around until somebody can figure out what to do with them. A nag makes really good fertilizer and even better glue!

Any time you open your mouth, be aware of what you are unleashing from the stable. Choose your words well. It is like grooming a horse. Make sure your words are useful and purposeful. They should not nag or kick wildly. Every time you open your mouth, know what you want to say and why. In other words, bridle your tongue!

My words put me in or take me out of the race!

YOU CANNOT RUN away from your problems. You can distance yourself in order to look back and assess your situation, but you can't get away from a persistent problem. A problem is like a tennis ball. It comes at you, you hit it to deflect it, but you cannot disarm a real problem with the swat of your hand. Until you are willing to sit in the middle of the problematic situation and pick it apart, piece by piece, until you get to the core, you will not be able to resolve it. It will remain a problem that grows from a little tennis ball into a giant missile. If you make one false move, it will explode!

A problem is a problem until you get to the root of the problem.

IN THE MIDDLE of panic, crisis, or confusion, it can be difficult to listen to what is said and not to what you hear. Even the slightest emotional upheaval will not only cloud your vision, it will also clog your ears. When we are upset, we hear with *fear muffs* on our ears. We hear with our broken hearts, our shattered egos, and our anger. At times like this, harmless little words take on great big meanings, and the smallest, most innocent gestures become life-threatening movements. You may feel like you are being attacked when you are actually being consoled. You may think you are being criticized when you are really being supported. If you know you are upset or feeling vulnerable, ask people what they are saying before you jump to a conclusion about what they have said.

Listen to what is said, not to what you hear.

———

YOU ARE BLESSED! It may not look or feel that way right now, but it's true. If you want to know how blessed you are, think back to a situation you thought was right for you and admit how wrong you were. At the time, you may not have realized you were growing. There was no way to know back then that something bigger and better was on the other side of something painful, ugly, and uncomfortable. Now look where you are and remember where you were.

Realize that where you are right now is not where you are going to be at some time in the near future. Whether you love it or hate it, your current condition is only temporary. Do your best. Do what you can. Give what you have to give, and remember, you are still growing. You are learning. In fact, you are earning new degrees of wisdom. Sure, you have some grief. You will have some fears. You might even have bouts of pain and sadness. However, just around the corner from where you are, you will be able to look back and see how truly blessed you are.

Whatever it is, I can do it for now.

The Valley of
O.P.P.

*Other people's problems, other people's priorities,
other people's principles, other people's people, can
get in our way, hold us back and take us off track
until we develop the strength to be honest with
ourselves.*

*T*hose who watch you march to your
death will salute you.

—*Nikki Giovanni*

WHAT IS THIS business of womanhood? Is it more than softness, beauty, motherhood, and girlfriends? Is it less than manhood? The same as manhood? And who said so? How do you know? What were your models of womanhood? Were they harsh? Cruel? Unheard? Tired? Abused? What images of womanhood do you hold? Aspire to?

Every morning you wake up a woman. What does it look like? How does it feel? Do you like it? Are you afraid of it? What is this business of womanhood? Is it sold? Can it be bought? Where do you find it? How do you keep it? Increase it? Was it given to you? Did you ask for it? Is it a blessing? Or a curse?

What is this business of womanhood? Do you work on it? Play with it? Does it work on you? Does it wear you out? Do you nurture it? Embrace it? How? When? Why? What is this business of womanhood? And how close does it come to being a child of God expressing the flesh from a feminine energy?

A woman's business is God's business!

THERE ARE TIMES when you innocently fall into things you cannot seem to get out of. Perhaps to keep the peace, you said you liked something or someone when you really didn't. Or maybe you said you would do something, knowing you didn't have the resources, hoping you could get them. It may have appeared that to tell the whole truth would have created a problem, so you deleted a few facts, altered a bit of the reality. You forgot to do something but you don't want anyone to know, so you try to cover your tracks. The innocence you had at the beginning will turn on you unless you tell the truth.

My daddy said, "Either you are lying or you are not lying." There is no such thing as a little lie, a good lie, or a necessary lie. You will be held accountable for everything that flows from your mouth. If you bring forth a lie, even a little lie, it will haunt you, and maybe even bite you. The process of life is truly impartial; it does not examine why we do what we do; it looks at what we did and holds us accountable for it. Rather than unleash a dishonest word and risk being bitten, don't say anything at all. Smile and nod. Say, "I can't offer an opinion or help now," or "Oops! Please forgive me, I forgot." When we develop a good habit of telling the truth to others, we avoid the damage we can ultimately cause by lying to ourselves.

When you know the truth, you must tell the truth!

DURING AN INTERVIEW, the host referred to me as "another self-help guru" after money, who had written "another self-help book" to get rich. As it fell from her mouth and in response to her tone of voice, my claws came out. While she continued to frame her question, with the lights and cameras shining in my face, I realized I had about thirty seconds to smooth my ruffled feathers. Breathing as deeply as I could, I realized she just didn't know. She was totally unaware of the time, prayer, and energy I put into my work. She had no idea of how many nights I sat up working, how many dates I passed up in order to work, how many meals I missed, or how seriously I take my work.

There will always be people who attempt to diminish or dismiss you. Some will not know any better, others simply don't care. A few will do it innocently. Others are consciously skeptical about, afraid of, or cynical about things they don't know about or care about. Some are afraid. None of that matters. What matters is your intent. What matters is your truth. What matters is what you know and feel about yourself. When I opened my mouth to respond, I lovingly reminded the host of the old African proverb, "It's not what people call me, it's what I answer to that counts."

I know who I Am!

VERY OFTEN WE place our trust in people, only to be disappointed. We must not allow those experiences to render us untrusting or untrustworthy. Trust is not something we give in response to what we get. Trust is not something we can acquire by anything we do. Trust is a decision we make within ourselves when we surrender control to God. If you believe you have been betrayed, used, taken for granted, or in some other way had your trust violated, decide now never to give up on people or yourself.

Everyone is held accountable for what they do. Not to you, but to life. Always remember, no matter what happens, or how bad you feel about it, or how much you don't like it, God knows exactly where you are and what you need. If you realize that your Creator is in control, there is never a reason to not trust people or yourself. ALL you have to do is trust that God will help you understand the value of your experiences . . . no matter what they look like.

Even when I'm hurt, I will trust the process!

WHEN YOU HEAR something that upsets you, ask yourself, "Where did I hear that before?" Who told me that I was no good? Unworthy? Not pretty? Find the people and the circumstances in your mind. Allow yourself to feel once again what you felt then. Trust that you can feel bad and recover. When you identify the people, forgive them, and forgive yourself for believing them.

In the midst of your forgiveness, a lot of confusion will show up. You may feel you are not smart enough, worthy enough, good enough to forgive yourself or others. It's okay, forgive anyway. You may believe that who you are or what you have done is too terrible to be forgiven. Forgive anyway. Fill your mind with forgiving thoughts. Speak forgiving words to yourself. Remember that your psyche is fragile. It is also powerful. You can heal, strengthen, empower yourself with a thought or a word, just as easily as you can be broken by the same.

I think forgiving thoughts. I speak forgiving words.

———

WE ARE ALL connected to the one Mind, one Life, one Power, one Spirit which is God. God created us all. God remains connected to us all. God knows everything there is to know about you and everybody else. When we really understand and embrace this concept, we will realize there is no need to run around telling people what somebody else has done. God already knows, and only S/He has the power to heal and correct.

Usually when we criticize, judge, or complain to people about other people, they are in no position to help us. In most cases, 80 percent of the people have their own people to complain about, and the other 20 percent don't care. Our problems with each other can be solved as soon as we give up the idea of how they "should" behave and what they "should" do. God is the only one who knows for sure who we are and our individual level of development. If we can remember the connection and recognize the need for healing, it becomes easy not to be angry or upset with people. They are minding their own life business. You are free to mind yours.

*The one Mind, one Life, one Power, one Spirit minds
us all.*

IT IS A BITTER pill to swallow, but betrayal in our lives is the outgrowth of fear in our minds. People do not necessarily betray us; sometimes we just set ourselves up to be a victim. We don't like to think about it. Very often we do not realize it. Yet the law works whether we recognize it or not. People often come into our lives to demonstrate that which we think and feel.

Each time we experience some form of betrayal, we are convinced about how weak, fragile, ill-equipped, or inadequate we are. We get to feel sorry for ourselves. We get to blame *others* for taking our power and we fall deeper into victimhood. We can't help ourselves when we are a victim. It's not our fault when we are a victim. We don't have to grow when we are a victim. Betrayal is just one of the tools the ego uses to make us victims and to ease God out of our lives.

You can get to the heart of betrayal by forgiving those who have hurt you before. You can ease betrayal out of your life by forgiving yourself for allowing others to make you a victim. You can turn all experiences of betrayal into steps toward empowerment by affirming over and over and over . . .

I Am not a victim!

THERE IS SOME bad news we all must accept, which is that everyone who starts out on the journey with us is not going to make it to the end. The good news is, you can be one of those who makes it. And there's more. No matter how you want to or try to help somebody else make it, you can only do what they allow you to do. But that's okay, because every good thing you do will come back to you better than you gave it. And that's not all.

On the journey, some people will fall behind you, and you will feel guilty for leaving them. Some people will fall in front of you, causing you to stumble. Still others will fall right next to you, scaring you half to death. Always keep in mind, if you stop on the journey to worry or doubt or fear, you will create a major obstacle. Others will then fall over you!

The bad news is, the journey is long and arduous. It is sometimes frightening. Sometimes lonely. All along the journey the path is littered with the bodies and skeletons of the fragile, the fallen, the forgotten. The good news is, whenever you are on the journey, you have only just begun.

I shall not fall off the path of the journey.

WHEN FRIENDS, FAMILY, and loved ones are in trouble, they will run to you for help. When you see them sinking into bad times, bad situations, bad habits, you feel it is your duty to help. The question we must ask ourselves is, how much help is too much help? When do our attempts to support, assist, encourage, or motivate become rescue mechanisms which keep people from learning their lessons and growing? In her book *Lessons in Truth,* Emilie Cady says, "One of the hardest things to do is stand still and watch somebody we love fall." Often we don't realize that in saving others we keep them from their lesson, and in doing so, we are actually encouraging the destructive behavior we want to save them from. There is a thin line between support and salvation, assistance and rescue. When we love someone or feel responsible to or for them, the line becomes blurred.

We all have appendages at the ends of our arms. They are called hands. Hands are not only for giving help; they are also for "self-help." Watch the patterns in which other people live. How they do what they do is clear indication of where they are with themselves. At times, it may seem to you, where a person is, is not a good place to be. However, you must also realize, they may not want to *get* out as badly as you want them to *be* out. When you rescue people, they cannot develop hard-working, capable hands of their own.

I see the good in you!

———

WHAT OTHER PEOPLE are doing or have done is not something you have to be concerned with or involved in. The issue you must address is, "What are you going to do?" You can feel badly, have empathy for what someone else is going through. You can feel their pain, know their concern, but the issue remains, what are you going to do?

There are times when people will tell us their problems, knowing "how we are." They haven't figured out how to come right out and ask for what they want, so they beat around the bush until we offer. In many situations, we can get pulled off track, out of line, away from our own issues in order to help, save, or rescue someone else. When people need support or assistance, we must allow them to ask for it. Once they do, we must make an honest assessment of what is or is not possible. We offer what we have rather than what we can get. We can also hear the pain, know their worry, and still choose what is best for us.

I hear your concern: "They won't ask for help!" They don't know how to ask for help!" And maybe that's the bigger issue. However, what other people can't do, what other people do not know how to do, is not something you must address to your own detriment. The issue you must address is, "What are you going to do?"

I don't know about you, but I know what I'm doing.

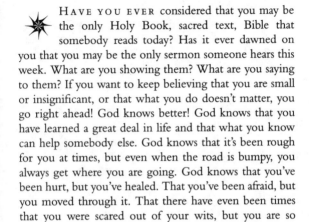

HAVE YOU EVER considered that you may be the only Holy Book, sacred text, Bible that somebody reads today? Has it ever dawned on you that you may be the only sermon someone hears this week. What are you showing them? What are you saying to them? If you want to keep believing that you are small or insignificant, or that what you do doesn't matter, you go right ahead! God knows better! God knows that you have learned a great deal in life and that what you know can help somebody else. God knows that it's been rough for you at times, but even when the road is bumpy, you always get where you are going. God knows that you've been hurt, but you've healed. That you've been afraid, but you moved through it. That there have even been times that you were scared out of your wits, but you are so tough, so powerful, so brilliant, you did not let that stop you. More than that, God knows people are always listening to what you say and what you do. In other words, God speaks to other people through you.

People watch me in order to hear God.

———

WHEREVER YOU ARE, at any time or place in your life, you will get what you need, by doing what you need to do. Others may not like or understand it, but you are on a mission. Your mission, is etched into the essence of your being. It is called DNA, *Discovering New Altitudes;* how else will you know what you can do unless you do it? People may warn you about the dangers, discourage you from taking chances. Just remember, most missions are wrought with danger. The falls and pitfalls you encounter toughen your hide, straighten your back, and coat your booty with Teflon. If you attempt to alter or change your mission simply to please other people, you will alter your DNA and retard your growth process.

By the way, your DNA is nobody's business but yours. You are not required to discuss your lessons or growth process with anyone unless you choose to. Your growth, new altitudes, and new dimensions will be fully recognizable. It is not your mission, assignment, or responsibility to live up to, down to, or according to anyone's opinion of you. When you realize this, you will also realize how far you can soar.

I'm on a mission.

I CAN REMEMBER being so afraid of what someone might say, I could not do what I needed to do. I thought about how upset they would be; how I would hurt their feelings; how angry they would be. I also thought I would lose their love or respect. In fear I did nothing. I don't think I am alone in this experience.

It is foolish to say we should not be concerned about the way in which our actions affect others. It is, however, equally foolish to make ourselves miserable, hold ourselves back, deny our own truth, to make someone else happy. A method I have discovered to relieve the stress of this type of experience is to forgive the person before I say or do anything. I forgive them for being angry or upset with me. I forgive them for anything they might say in anger. I forgive them for not honoring my needs and my truth. Then I say what I must say, do what I must do.

Forgiveness keeps the channels of communication open. It eliminates stress and clarifies the truth. Honest forgiveness keeps you from being upset or derailed by the words or actions of another. You have already imagined the worst and forgiven it; there is no way you can be hurt or shocked. The most important aspect of forgiving, at the start, is the realization that you cannot lose anyone's love. Either they love you and honestly want you happy or they don't! Now, forgive yourself for believing what you must do for you means you cannot be loved.

I move forward with forgiveness.

JOY IS WHAT we are, not what we must get. Joy is the realization that all we want or need in life has been etched into our souls. Periods of success followed by long periods of unhappiness and dissatisfaction are not the natural order of life. We are not put here to suffer and then die. Yet it seems that we are unable to sustain an even flow of pleasure and ease in our daily affairs and relationships. Things never seem to add up when we make the tally of pleasure and pain, ease and difficulty, good times and bad times. Perhaps this is because we are using the wrong measurements.

Joy, not pleasure; joy, not ease; joy, not happiness. Joy is an internal mechanism which keeps us on an even plane as we move through life. Joy gives us the ability to move through an unpleasant situation, knowing that once we make it through, it is over. Joy reminds us of what we need to learn in order to experience longer periods of joy.

Joy helps us to see not what we are "going through" but what we are "growing to," a greater sense of understanding, accomplishment, and enlightenment. Joy reveals to us the calm at the end of the storm, the peace that surpasses the momentary happiness of pleasure. If we keep our mind and heart centered on joy, the joy of growing, of knowing, of living, joy becomes a state of mind, not an elusive preoccupation we choose, only to have it slip through our fingers over and over.

I Am joy!

WHAT WOULD HAPPEN if you let your dream come true in front of a million people??

What would people think about you, say to you if you started to have fun in public? What do you think people would think if suddenly you became very successful, very wealthy, very powerful right before their eyes? Whatever you think people would think is probably the thing that keeps you from doing it. Most of us are not willing to risk making people mad at us.

It may be difficult to believe, but the people around us want us to succeed. They may not act that way. They may never say a word. Some of them probably don't realize it, but it is a lot harder for them to watch you suffer and struggle than it is for you to succeed. We often get in the way of our own success by worrying about what other people will think. In the worst case, some of us hold ourselves back in fear of leaving or losing those close to us. We are afraid to outshine them. We think it will make them angry or uncomfortable.

Living your life to its fullest potential is a fun thing to do. Those around you can watch and cheer you on. If they watch carefully, they can learn something. If they love you, they too will benefit from your success.

Let's have some fun.

LIFE IS DEPENDING on you to shine. Life is waiting for you to bloom. Life is waiting for you to glorify it. Please don't let life down. Be sure not to allow other people to "should" on you. Folks are always so ready to let you know what you "should be" or "should not be" doing, they get very little done in their own lives. If your mother, father, sister, brother, friend is so sure of what you should be doing, let them do it. Remember, good advice is not always free. You pay dearly for it with little pieces of your life and your self. It may be challenging to move beyond the expectations and demands others have of or for you, but remember, a good challenge strengthens your muscles.

Please! Do not should on me!

IT IS SO easy to get caught up in being who others want you to be. It is even easier to convince yourself that who you are is not enough. If we are not careful and conscious, we can spend a good part of life acting out roles and expectations rather than living who we are. "Who am I?" is the question we should start the day with. Know that you are not your name, job, or level of education. You are not who your mother, father, sister, brother, husband, children say you are. You are not your dress size, hair length, number of credit cards. Who am I? For some of us it is a frightening question. To know who we are means we must move beyond the names and labels. It means we must shake off restrictions and limitations. To know ourselves is to love and accept ourselves as divine children of God. To know "who I am" means having no more excuses to be anything else for anyone else other than the Divine Father/Mother.

I Am who I Am.

SPEAKING FOR MYSELF, I have been made to feel responsible for so much, for so long, there was a part of me that believed I had to do it all. No matter what happened or who it happened to, I had to fix it. I had to fix my mother, my children, my friends, things that happened at work, and most other things that came along. When I couldn't fix it, I felt bad. Then I realized that even when I did fix it, I felt bad. I resented being responsible for having to fix so much and so many. As the resentment and exhaustion built up, I was forced to take a new approach. That is when I realized that by fixing everything on the outside, I was avoiding looking at those things I believed were wrong with me. As long as I could fix other things, I did not feel broken. As long as I could fix other people, I felt whole.

As women, we owe it to ourselves and life to assist, support, and serve others. We must remember, however, that we cannot give what we do not have. Give to yourself first! Do what you can because you want to, because of love. Never act from a false sense of responsibility. Fixing people and things is only a temporary relief which masks what we really believe about our self. In the end, we must come back to the mirror of self. Take time to heal the internal wounds that make you believe you are not enough. Once this is done, you will know when you have done enough!

I've done enough!

WE TRY TO make everything all right for other people. When they hurt, we want to stop their pain. When they need, we do everything in our power to ensure that the need is met. When they make mistakes, we fix them and, in some cases, cover them up. We set ourselves up to be leaned on, but when people lean too hard or too much, we get angry. We feel used.

Some of us have a need to be needed. We derive self-value and self-worth from the things we do for others. We feel good when we are "doing." When the doing stops, we need more than people are able or willing to give us. Unfortunately, in the doing process we often lose sight of ourselves and our needs.

Remember that you set the standards for how you will be treated. People will treat you the exact way you treat yourself. If you don't want to be a crutch, don't set yourself up. Be good to you. Take time for yourself. Rest. Play. Shower yourself with affection, support, and gifts. Don't be afraid to be unavailable. Train yourself to know when to say no.

I have something to do for myself.

WHEN YOU MAKE a decision and a commitment to do something good for yourself, it is like dropping a pebble in a pond. It has a rippling effect. Energy vibrations are sent out into the universe that touch people and places you may not see. The firmer the decision, the stronger the frequency and wider the range of things that will be reached. Those things are being prepared to receive, support, and assist you in honoring your decision. The ripples closest to you may make you uncomfortable. They may rattle you a bit. That's okay! It is bound to happen. A decision will usually have a long-term and far-reaching effect. However, if it is for your good, all you have to do is stand firm. All that you need will find its way to you, and the unnerving ripples around you will go away soon.

I Am standing firm in this decision!

ARE YOU LIVING your life or are you living your mother's life? Perhaps you are living the life that your father told you to live. Maybe your life was custom-built for you by your husband, your sister, or the "system." Does your life suit your needs? Is it too big for you? Is it too small for you? Is your life satisfactory? Do you live in your life, or around it? Do you dare do what you want to do, or are you consumed doing what you are told you *have to* do?

It is very easy to get stuck living your life for others, doing what they want you to do in order for them to get what they need. There is a very delicate balance between *my life, our lives,* and *your life.* When you are not clear about who you are, what you need, and what you want, the balance can be tipped against your favor. If you need to reclaim your life and live it, be sure to do it! You can accomplish this by taking time for yourself to take care of yourself. You must also be sure to let people know what you need, and to be willing to say no to what they need without feeling guilty about it.

I have a life that I want to live.

THERE ARE FEW things more painful or difficult than watching a loved one go through difficulty. Chances are they will give you a
blow-by-blow account of their pending demise. It is even
worse when they say nothing at all and you discover how
bad they are really doing from outside sources. Your first
instinct is to rush to help them, to give them what you
think they need to put an end to their misery. You hurt
because they hurt, and you want to stop hurting with
them and for them. In these situations, there are a few
things you want to remember—

1. It's not your issue.
2. Don't get stuck in other people's stuff.
3. When people get tired of suffering and struggling,
   they stop.

Does this mean you should not help out a friend or
loved one in need? Of course not! Do what you can
without putting yourself in jeopardy. However, you must
also realize that, in some cases, people will suffer because
they know someone understands. As long as they believe
someone understands their misery, they will believe they
have a right to be miserable! When you run into people
who are perpetually miserable, your job is to pray for
them, hold them in the light of your mind, send them lots
of love and . . . get out of the way!

Misery does not need company!

The Valley of Comeuppance

Teaches us that we are all held accountable to the universe for everything we think, say, and do. The energy of dominant thoughts and words creates conditions in our lives.

*W*hile I know myself as a creation of God, I am also obligated to realize and remember everyone else and everything else are also God's creation.

—*Maya Angelou*

SOMETIMES IT'S GOT to get worse before it gets better. Sometimes it is not until the muck and mire are so deep, so thick, that we realize there has got to be a change. As long as we have little problems, we are willing and able to maneuver our way around. When the challenges are small, we can find a quick fix, a means of deliverance, without realizing there is a deeper problem, a bigger issue which requires healing.

Healing is not like fixing. Fixing is doing whatever we can to cover up, disguise, or eliminate the problem . . . temporarily. Healing cuts to the core, goes to the bone, as a means of eliminating the cause of the problem . . . forever. Band-Aids fix. They cover the problem up. Keep it clean and out of sight. When something is healing, it will ooze, cause pressure, or hurt. Stitches will fix, close up the problem, make it bearable. If, however, there is an infection under the stitches, the wound must be opened; the infection must be cleaned out before there is any relief. Healing is a great deal more painful than fixing. But think of it this way; once there is a healing, the problem goes away for good.

I Am in a healing process!

I ONCE READ that struggle, suffering, and conflict are like magnets that draw us closer to God.
It is not until we feel totally helpless, confused,
sometimes desperate, that we become willing or able to
turn to the awesome power of life and living our Creator
offers us. We may know God exists. We may understand
our connection to God. Yet it seems that it is not until we
are down or on the way down that we invite God's presence and power into our life. It doesn't have to be this
way. God not only offers emergency care, S/He is a source
of preventive care.

Your Creator always wants the best for you. Your
Creator has a mission, plan, and purpose designed just for
you. Sometimes when things are going our way, when
they are comfortable or easy, we forget about God. We
get off track, out of line, we move away from the plan,
mission, and purpose. Difficulties in life are not meant to
break us or break us down. Our greatest challenge may be
a simple reminder, the only way we will remember that
there is a Higher Authority to whom we are accountable.
The real challenge we face is to keep God, God's word,
and God's way in the forefront of our mind—in good
times as well as bad.

I Am a magnet for God's good!

God cannot fix the mess we create.
What God can do, will do, and does all the time
is give us the courage and presence of mind
to do whatever needs to be done
to rectify our errors.
What we must do is ask for guidance, and trust
it will be okay.

God will guide me through it.

LINKING THE FUTURE to the pain of the past does not allow the light to come in. Today always offers new light; however, when you hold on to what you believe about yesterday, that belief will not allow you to explore new possibilities. Beliefs demand loyalty. If you try to move away from the things you believe in, they will punish you. The belief will make you feel guilty. Guilt is your punishment for abandoning what you believe.

Spirit is the only power which can intervene between the pain of the past and the light of the future. You must rely on the spirit of truth, love, peace, joy, and freedom to change your beliefs and free you from all guilt. What happened yesterday does not have to happen today unless you believe it must. Until you have enough faith to allow the power and presence of spirit to infuse your mind and change your beliefs, you will continue on the path of yesterday's painful darkness.

Spirit brings the light of new beliefs.

UNFORTUNATELY, MOST OF us have no idea of what the solution looks like because we are too busy fighting the problem. For some reason, it seems that we are prone to pay more attention to what we don't want. When difficulties and challenges confront us, the mind naturally shifts to what we cannot do, do not want to do, fear doing. In response to the dynamic power of the mind, we get more of the very thing we don't want. As the anxiety, fear, and resistance grow in our mind, the situation appears to become worse.

Any spiritual teacher will tell students, "Never focus on the problem; focus on the solution." In difficult times, the mind seems to take on a will of its own, reminding us of the possible horror we face. How are we to free ourselves of the pictures in the mind long enough to see the desired outcome? The answer is simple: go through the darkness to the light. The difficulty of any situation is not the situation; it is our resistance to it. At the time of our greatest challenge, we must allow the mind to go all the way through to the end. Give yourself permission to see the horror, feel the fear, anticipate the pain. When you've done that, it's over. Chances are if you let your mind go to where you don't want to be, you will never have to take your body through it. You can go through the problem mentally; you get a better picture of what the solution looks like. From that position, you can silently affirm:

I can do this!

EVERY NEW PHASE of life is walking up to a locked door. Some doors are poorly constructed, with locks that are easy to pick. These doors are easily opened. Other doors are very big and very well constructed, with big locks that cannot be opened without a key. Even when you have the key, a big door can still be hard to open. You have to push a little harder, and once you get it open, you must be very careful that the door doesn't close on your fingers or slam shut before you can get in.

Difficulties in life represent doors you must go through. The doors are not there to keep you out. They are there to prepare you for what you will encounter on the other side. On the other side of the door are the things that you have been looking for, waiting for, and asking for. On the other side of the door are all the things that you have been prepared to have by opening all the other doors. Why do you care if you have to push, kick, or knock the door down? You've got the keys: faith, confidence, and prayer. The only thing you have to do is remember, big doors with heavy-duty locks are used to protect very valuable things!

Big doors lead to big blessings!

E VERY MUSCLE, TISSUE, and cell in your body today is different than it was seven years ago. Every strand of hair you have today is different. Every toenail and fingernail you have today are not the same ones you had just a few months ago. Today, you are totally different in every physiological sense than you were three, five, or seven short years ago. The question is, how different is your mind?

Each moment, your physical body changes without any input on your part. Your mind, however, is a completely different issue. You must work to change your mind. You must be willing to release past pains, past regrets, and ancient resentments. You must be willing to let go of hostility, anger, and judgments about experiences and people. The people in your past, like you, have also changed. They have new hair, new tissues, new cells, new toenails and fingernails! It is up to you, however, to see them in a new light . . . even when it looks like they are doing the same thing. The only thing that will keep you stuck in the past with old experiences, useless emotions, and worn-out habits is your mind. Fortunately, you have the ability to change your mind to match everything else that is new about you.

You are renewed! Now change your mind!

◤ MAYBE WHAT YOU really need is a spiritual diet! A spiritual diet will cut down on the excess weight you carry around in your soul. The weight of people who have disappointed you or hurt you. The weight of things you should have done, could have done, or wanted to do, but couldn't bring yourself to do. As a matter of fact, that weight around your middle could be those people you've been hanging around or allowing to hang onto you. The heaviness in your legs could be all those things you convinced yourself you were not smart enough, good enough, or ready enough to do. That sluggish, heavy feeling you have in your heart might be your dreams, goals, and fantasies. You haven't put them to use, so they've turned to weight, spiritual weight which has your whole life weighed down.

Yes! I believe a spiritual diet is exactly what you need! You can start right now with a heaping portion of forgiveness smothered in surrender. You will also need a big helping of laughter three to four times a day. Next, you must begin each day with prayer, followed by a dose of gratitude. For the next six to eight weeks, sprinkle everything with faith, wash it down with courage, and let your dessert be a swig of confidence. If you follow these directions with all your heart, you will experience a miraculous weight loss.

Lose a little weight and worry with a spiritual diet.

———

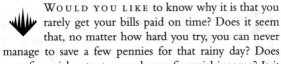 WOULD YOU LIKE to know why it is that you rarely get your bills paid on time? Does it seem that, no matter how hard you try, you can never manage to save a few pennies for that rainy day? Does your financial output exceed your financial income? Is it all making you crazy? The solution is really quite simple. You must heal your lack of consciousness.

As long as you are pinching, scratching, struggling with money, it will fight you, avoid you, and operate in a diminished capacity in your life. When it looks like you don't have enough, stop looking! Start writing the check and praising the universe for divine substance. Money is not in low supply. However, if you believe there is not enough to go around, no money will come your way. Remember, God is your Source and Supply. God is never broke. God is never late. God showers abundant riches on those who open the doors of their mind with trust, faith, praise, and a solid budget which includes giving, sharing, and receiving.

I lack no good thing. I Am open to abundance.

ALL OF US have things in our lives we would rather the world not know about. Every living being knows things about who they are which they prefer not to broadcast. No person living has not done or said something which, if they had it to do again, they would do it another way. We are not alone in the darkness of our habits, personality, mistakes, or poor choices. Yet when these experiences are revealed, we often feel alone, ashamed, guilty.

Life will not allow you to be guilty forever! No one, not even you, deserves to be punished forever! When the darkness about you or your life is revealed, rejoice! Know that it is coming up in order to move out. When darkness is revealed, it means that our consciousness is moving toward the light. It is a reflection of our inner readiness to release the past and move forward with clarity. Darkness coming to the light is a good thing. It is a God thing. And God never asks us to do more than we can, before we are able. Remember, the light of God will reveal anything unlike itself. The closer you walk toward the spirit of God, the more likely it is that your darkness will come to light.

I can see the light before me!

FEAR IS LIKE a shot of white sugar directly into the brain cells. It causes the mind to race. In fear, the mind makes you believe that something is gaining on you, about to overtake you, and that the worst thing possible and imaginable is about to happen to poor little old you. Fear is an intoxicant. It makes you high. But just as with all highs, there comes the moment when you crash.

Coming down from a fear-induced high means you will confront the very thing you were trying to get away from. All the things you kept in the back of your mind, believing you could not face, you must now face. As you crash into the situation or person feared, you may feel the need to lie your way out; fight your way around it; or simply tuck your pride between your legs and beg for mercy. If you are a student of life, on the journey of evolution and empowerment, there are two things you must do when you are in fear: (1) Breathe! (2) Surrender!

When you are in fear, take several long, deep breaths. This will help you stay in your body so you can hear your divine guidance. In order to hear what you must do, you must surrender everything you think might happen. In this way, you make way in your mind for what is divinely ordained to happen. Fear is simply a signal that you are about to embark upon a mystery of some kind. But life is a series of mysteries, isn't it?

I surrender! I surrender! I surrender!

WALLY AMOS ONCE said, "If you're going through hell, don't stop to take pictures!" But that's exactly what we do, isn't it? We maintain a mental catalog of every detail of what has happened. When the situation is over, we show off our mental pictures by telling the story over and over, embellishing the worst details. It creates pain in the brain and drama in life. We hate it, but we do it, unconsciously.

When we hold on to and mentally relieve painful past experiences, we create enemies. There is always someone to be leery of; someone or something to watch out for; what we fail to realize is that the kind of mental darkness in the back of our minds creates an *"enemy in me."*

Within you there is an awesome power, a divine intelligence, that is accessible and available, wherever you are. It is a guiding light. Unfortunately, this light can't shine when we keep ourselves surrounded in dark memories. When a photographer takes film into a darkroom, the negative images are exposed to light. The light creates a new image. Only when we expose the negativeness in our brain to light, can we create a new picture in our lives.

Let there be light!

Would you lie on forms you were submitting to God?
Would you keep God's change if S/He miscounted?
Would you gossip about God?
Would you criticize God?
Would you invite God over when your house is a mess
or
when you have mud on your face,
curlers in your hair, and morning breath?
No!
Then why do you do it to the world and to the people
which God created?

I see God in all things and all people.

LET US SAY someone has hurt your feelings. What does that really mean? What do you really feel? Feelings of being attacked, betrayed, rejected, unsupported today are usually the memories of yesterday's anger, fear, and helplessness. The challenge is to figure out what we feel; how it feels; even more important, why we feel the way we do. For many of us, it began in childhood. Yesterday's pain becomes what we "feel" today.

There is no part of the physical anatomy called "feelings." The response we have to any given situation is a reflection of what we are telling our selves about what is going on. If, as children, we believed we were unloved, unworthy, unimportant, we will continue to "feel" that way in response to whatever happens in our lives. It is an old memory wearing a new dress. But big girls have the power to change their clothes whenever they choose to do so.

The next time an old memory shows up in a new experience, do not allow it to hurt you. Take a deep breath before you say or do anything. Gently ask yourself, "What is really going on here?" "What am I remembering?" Give yourself time to get clear about where you are in your thoughts. Only with clarity about what is going on inside of you will you begin to "feel" better about what you experience outside of you.

Yesterday can't hurt me today.

MANY OF US approach life from a perspective of deficit. We try to move forward on the premise of what we *cannot* do, honestly believing we can build upon this kind of foundation. As hard as we try, there is always something we cannot do because we believe that we do not have what we need to build. We think the problem is the conditions in which we live, the situations in which we find ourselves, or the people involved in the situations and circumstances. We haven't got a clue that our language defines our problems and re-creates our reality!

Take some time to listen to what you say over the course of the next few days. When you hear yourself say, "I'm struggling to get by!" "It's so hard out here!" "I'm just trying to make it!" remind yourself that words become conditions. Situations may be dark or dismal, but you can always speak about the good you can find in them. Conditions in your life may be challenging and difficult, but you have the ability to speak encouraging words to yourself. People may treat you unfairly, unjustly, or in the most unloving ways, but you reserve the right to counteract people with words. You're doing just fine! Hey! You keep getting better day by day! This is not as bad as it seems! You can do this! I know you can! These are just a few of the profitable things you can tell yourself to move beyond the confines of any deficit.

You can say what you want to see and be!

———

GOD, THE SPIRIT of life, will always meet you where you are. Never pushing, never forcing, but always reflecting back to you the level of your own understanding. If you believe in a harsh, punishing God, that is who you will meet in your time of need. If you believe in a loving, compassionate God, S/He will be your guide. If you believe in a partial, unjust God, you will experience the outgrowth of that belief if and when you turn to God for support. When you believe in a powerless or limited God, who only hears when S/He wants to hear, you will have experiences which will confirm exactly what you believe. Your beliefs and perceptions don't change the true nature of God, but they do determine the experience you will have when you seek God. One of the most important principles to remember in life is, you always get exactly what you expect!

The bigger, better, more powerful the belief, the bigger, better, more productive the experience!

DIFFICULTIES PREPARE YOU for victory. Disease prepares you for health. Confusion prepares you for clarity. Hopelessness prepares you for purpose. Failure prepares you for success. Poverty prepares you for prosperity. Criticism prepares you for acceptance. Pain prepares you for joy. Anger prepares you for forgiveness. Ignorance prepares you for truth. Loneliness prepares you for love. Love prepares you to stand face to face with God. God is the one who sends whatever it is you need to be prepared. It is called healing. Only God can heal you.

God is in the healing business.

THERE IS ALWAYS the temptation to look at your circumstances to justify your position in life. "I'm like this because . . ." "My parents made me this way!" "I can't do any better because . . ." Many people fall into the trap of believing they are the way they are because of the circumstances in their lives. What few of us realize is that the circumstances of your life reveal who you are, not what has happened to you!

We cannot escape the truth that every experience, every relationship, and every aspect of our environment is in direct correlation to how we think and what we think. It is not the other way around. Circumstances do not make you unless you think yourself down to them. If you allow history, an unsupportive environment, or unsupportive people to hold you back, it is your choice! A choice to believe you are stuck in the circumstances! A circumstance is a creation of the mind that can always be changed with a belief and a thought. Anytime you are ready to get out of your present circumstances, you can get out! The key is to fight the temptation to believe you cannot!

A circumstance is a mental creation!

Y O U   D O   N O T come to life totally helpless and lost. When you are born, the general direction of your journey is very clear. You have a gender. You are expressing a particular ethnic heritage. You are born in a particular location under a specific set of circumstances. These are the general parameters of your journey. It is up to you to determine the specific route you will take and what your final destination will be.

What you do with what you have been given in life is entirely up to you. You are free to move in any direction you choose, at any time you like. Keep in mind that once you start the journey you can change your mind about the direction in which you want to go. You are free to go up or down, forward or backward at any time and at your own pace. If you ever get lost or lose your footing on the journey, all you have to do is get in contact with the One who sent you here in the first place! S/He will be more than willing to help you get back onto the path of your choice.

Even if you have a map, you may need help reading it!

YOU CAN GET so caught up in being miserable that you will not see your blessing when it comes! You can become so addicted to having crisis in your life that the minute one crisis is resolved, you are on the lookout for the next one! It is very easy to miss the perfectly delightful experiences and moments of peace or joy when you are preoccupied with all of the possible tragedies that could befall you. It is quite possible that you have many of the bad situations you have in your life because you pay so much attention to them, they feel welcomed. It is also reasonable to believe that if you stopped paying so much attention to the bad things, they would feel neglected and go away! If you don't believe it, try it just to see if it works.

When a bad situation gets no attention, it becomes a better situation!

ARE YOU AFRAID of your feelings? Perhaps it is because you expect to be *caught* by surprise, or to be *thrown* into the middle. Maybe you've been *pushed* out front only to be *knocked* off your feet. How many times have you *fallen* in love only to have your heart *broken* when you were *kicked* in the face by someone you loved? When was the last time you were *stabbed* in the back by someone you trusted with your heart? If you think about it, we use such violent terms to describe our emotional experiences, it is understandable that we are afraid to open ourselves to the full range of emotions we are capable of experiencing.

Your feelings are the gauge of your life. How you express them or repress them determines the degree of your mental, emotional, and spiritual health. When we attach drama and fear to our emotional experiences, we are prone to shut down in order to protect ourselves. What you want to remember when you are on the telephone, crying your eyes out with your girlfriend, is that no matter what you feel, it is perfect! Your most heart-wrenching and painful experience is just as much part of the process of life as all the good things you have experienced. And, no matter what happens to you, it is crucial that you keep your heart open and experience your emotions. It is only when you can feel that you know you are truly and fully alive.

Be open to feel it. Use your power to heal it!

THE REWARD YOU receive for a job well done is getting a bigger, harder job to do. Many of us believe that once we demonstrate how strong, how good, how smart we are, life should give us a break. We believe we should be home free. Nothing could be further from the truth about the way life works. The trees with the strongest branches and deepest roots are those that have withstood the heavy winds and stormy weather, season after season.

You must never become tired of reaching, stretching, growing, and becoming better and better. The old folks called it "moving from glory to glory!" You must always keep in mind that the more you know and the more you can do, the more you will be called upon. Yes, you have a right to be tired. Yes, you are entitled to a much-deserved rest. Once you get rested, get ready! Life is going to bring you a big task to perform, a deep mystery to resolve, a harder job to work on, and a greater victory than you have ever had before.

Best to better! Biggest to bigger! Victory to victory is the journey of the great!

DEAR SELF,

If you have it to give, give it! If you know what to say, say it! If you know what needs to be done, do it! If there is some place you want to go, go now! If there is something you want to do, do it! What are you waiting for? Haven't you figured out yet that you are the only one who can do what you do, the way you do it? Don't you realize that the world is waiting for you?

Give it! Say it! Do it! Now!

WHAT IS IT going to take before we realize how absolutely wonderfully special and blessed we are? We are a human *being*, which means we are endowed with everything we need to master this thing called life. We are not a human *becoming* or a human *could be*. We are *being* now all that we are born capable of being. Why are we acting like there is something else we need? Isn't life enough?

Life is all that humans need to be in!

DEAR GOD,

Please remind me that my days are num-
bered. Teach me that my time here in this life is
precious so that I will not waste it. Help me to recognize
how precious every moment is so that I spend it doing
those things that will bring me closer to You. In the time
I have left, please teach me how to serve You, Dear God.
Teach me how to give joyously, share willingly, and love
totally. Remind me that I cannot serve in greed, doubt,
fear, or anger. Fill my soul with Your light, so that Your
bountiful blessings will shine through my soul into the
world. Each day that I awake, I pray that You will be
present in my thoughts, my words, and all of my deeds. I
ask that every moment that I have left in this life be a
channel through which some measure of Your love and
light may reach those with whom I come into contact.

A closer walk with God is time well spent!

The Valley of Purpose and Intent

Teaches us to be clear about our purpose and how to make a commitment to that purpose.

Don't no good come outta bad.
Can't get much bad outta real good.
Hold on to your good, your essence, until
you find the people and situations that
match it.

—MARITA GOLDEN, AND DO REMEMBER ME

THE QUESTION IS, what are you willing to do to get what you say you want? Are you willing to discipline your mind and your mouth? Are you willing to get up early, stay up late, and work hard all the hours between? Are you willing to work for free? Are you willing to do it with excellence? Are you willing to do it even when your best friend shakes her head, laughs at you, and tells you that you are crazy?

The question is, what are you willing to give up to get what you say that you want? Are you willing to give up bad habits, negative thinking, and negative people? Are you willing to take a risk and put your butt on the line when all the signs indicate that you are totally insane? Are you willing to stand up for yourself? To speak up for yourself? Are you willing to walk away from the people who will be very upset when you stand up and speak up? Are you willing to walk away from everything you now know to get to something and someplace you can only hope will be what you want it to be?

The question is, who are you willing to be? Are you willing to be a free and independent thinker? Are you willing to be the one who calls the shots? Are you willing to have fun? Are you willing to live in total peace and joy? Are you willing to have fun and joy in total peace all by yourself, if necessary? As long as you can find one excuse not to answer these questions affirmatively, you will never have what you say you want.

Have all that you are willing to have!

IF YOU KNOW that your life is a journey and if you want to make it to your divine destination, you must learn to travel light! Shake off all of the *nosey-know-it-alls* who try to convince you that they know what you need and how you should go about getting it! Throw away all of the *chronic-complaining-criticizers* who have never done anything except complain or criticize! Tear yourself away from the *whimpering-whiners* who have excuses for not doing all the things they have not done! Shake yourself free from the *low-life-lovers* who make many promises and keep few commitments! Unpack the abrasive attitudes, addictive appetites, belittling burdens, conflicting confusion, and frivolous fears that you have packed away in the crevices of your heart and mind. Pack a tidbit of truth, a capsule of courage, a fistful of faith, and a pocketful of prayer, and be on your way!

Pack light! Make the journey easy!

THERE IS ONE sure way to know that you are doing exactly what God wants you to do: you will be at peace. Not every day, not all the time, but even in the midst of hard times and confusion you will feel good about what you are doing. Even when it seems like you are getting nowhere, you will know there is absolutely nothing else on earth you can do other than what you are doing. It's called being on purpose.

There will be times when you will want to walk away but you won't. You can't. Perhaps the money will not show up fast enough. You will figure out what you can do with the money you have. Maybe things you need will not be there when you think you need them. You will figure out how to do without them. You may even convince yourself that there is something bigger, better, more rewarding, you can be doing with your time. Just when you are about to give up, you will get a second wind, some much needed help that will keep you going just a little longer.

When you are doing what God wants you to do, the money won't matter. You will be willing to stick it out in the bad times. You will ignore the people who tell you you can't or that you are crazy. You will be so intent on finding the happiness and success you know you deserve, you will be at peace. In peace, you find God's purpose for you.

Your peace is God's pleasure.

Pssssst! I HAVE something very important to tell you. I know you are busy building a life for yourself. I realize you are working real hard to make it, to follow your dreams, and to realize some sense of personal satisfaction, but what I have to say is very important, otherwise, I wouldn't bother you. You may want to consider what I have to say before you make another move or take another step. It is something you probably know but may have forgotten to consider in all of your plans. Or maybe you have considered it but couldn't figure out how it works. What I want you to know is, unless you ask God what it is S/He wants you to do, you will never know! Once you ask, listen to your heart for the answer and watch for signs. In the meantime, if you don't get an answer, that is the answer!

God has something for you to do!

———

THE BEST WAY to create abundance in your life is to surround yourself with abundance. What you see, you become! If you want to be wealthy, go to the places wealthy people go. Do the things that wealthy people do. If your first thought is, "I can't afford to do that!" you will know why you do not have wealth and abundance—you don't think abundantly.

Abundant thoughts attract abundant experiences! A wealthy consciousness attracts wealth! If you don't know what wealthy people do—study! Read what the wealthy people read. Eat what wealthy people eat. Walk through wealthy environments. Save some money. Invest some money. And please, don't make the mistake of thinking that wealth has anything to do with race! Abundance is an attitude. Wealth is a consciousness. You can create an abundantly wealthy lifestyle right now, where you are, with what you have, by bringing yourself into alignment with wealth. The best part of learning to be wealthy and live abundantly when you are not is that you will know exactly what to do when the wealth shows up!

See wealth in your midst, have wealth in your life!

Money, fine clothes, fancy cars, public acknowledgment
are no substitute for purpose.
When you know your purpose,
you know you are about the business
of what you have come here to do;
you are on purpose.
With purpose,
you have vision.
With purpose,
you have clarity.
With purpose,
you have the support, power, and
blessings of the universe
at your disposal.

My purpose gave birth to me.

YOU KNOW EVERYTHING will turn out just fine. Even if it doesn't feel like it right now, you know, "This too shall pass." The question then becomes, what do you do in the meantime? How do you wait in peace and faith? Well, did you breathe? Go ahead. Take a few long, deep breaths, inhaling through the nose, exhaling through the mouth, making the sound "Ahhhh." That sound represents the name of God. That's your power. Don't forget to use it. Go ahead; breathe.

Did you pray? Did you confess from your heart to God what you are thinking, feeling, wanting right now? You know that prayer can get into places you can't; prayer changes things. Even better, prayer changes people, and people change things. So go ahead and pray.

Have you surrendered?? Have you given up your way to the will and the way of Spirit? Are you willing to give up control, realizing that whatever you want is probably far less than Spirit will do, once you get out of the way? If you are not breathing, if you haven't prayed, if you are not willing to surrender, it's no wonder you are in a panic.

I do know what to do.

SOME OF US want life to be like a refrigerator. We want to be preserved just as we are and to be kept crisp around the edges. We do not want to wilt or melt under the pressures of life. We want to stand in our own little space, keeping everything else in its own space so that we will not be contaminated.

I think life is like a toaster. You've got to be pushed down in order to pop up and meet the demands of life. You have to get done before you will know what to do. For most of us, unless we have a little heat under our bottoms, we will sit around and get stale. Also remember, when cold, hard things are placed on a hot piece of toast, they melt and fade away, but when you cast your bread on the waters of life, it will return to its place of origin multiplied.

The heat of light fuels the spirit to live!

YOU ARE A guest in this house. Life has invited you in for a while. You don't know how long you are going to be here, so while you are here you must be on your best behavior. Walk and talk softly so you don't disturb other people. Those who need to know you are here, will know. If you use something, put something back in its place. If you make a mess, clean up after yourself. Don't wait to be told what to do. If you see something that needs to be done, do it. Do it with joy and love, and please do it well. Try to leave this place in better shape than it was when you got here.

Be mindful not to whine or complain too much. Speak your mind when necessary, but do it with respect and in love. As you move through life's house, be sure to look nice. Not fancy or flashy, just neat and clean. It brings others great joy to see you look good. Above all else, always be grateful for every little thing life does for you. She could have invited anyone else, but you are someone special, so She chose you.

I Am a guest in life's house.

IN LIFE THERE are two kinds of hunters: the kind that hunts for prey and the kind that hunts for people. The difference between hunting for prey and for people is that the hunter traps the prey and kills it. The spirit captures people so that they can live. There is only one way to prevent yourself from becoming prey to the hunters; that is to allow yourself to be captured by the Spirit of life. Spirit is always on the lookout for those who really want to live. The spirit of truth! The spirit of peace! The spirit of joy and the spirit of love are searching for souls right now. Once you are caught, your life will never be the same!

Get caught up in the spirit of life!

DEAR SELF,
I will not assault my mind or spirit
with a lengthy discourse about the horror against
or the virtues of being a woman.
I will begin right now, where I am, getting to those
places
I can go if I choose to.
I will begin with the first step according to spiritual law,
doing all that is required for healing, transformation, and
evolution.
"You must bare your soul," they say.
But I know,
you cannot clean the fish and leave the water dirty.
I am the fish. I am everlasting substance.
The waters are my emotions.
They must be cleaned.
I must let the water out and fill myself
with new thoughts, new feelings, and new energy.
Then and only then will I be able to feed
the multitudes.

It is time to cleanse my mind.

There is something phenomenal going on!
I'm not quite sure what it is, and quite frankly,
I don't care!
I simply know, whatever it is,
it will be great!
It has to do with change, healing, growth, and evolution.
And
It has to do with women.
If I were pressed, I would put it in words like this:
There are changes taking place in the hearts and minds of
women
that are going to rock the world!
Women are changing their minds about who they are;
and what their role will be in the world order.
Women are learning to be responsible for the healing
of their mental, physical, emotional, and spiritual selves.
Women are learning to love themselves and each other.
Most of all, women are evolving to the point
where they are no longer willing to accept crap
from themselves or from anyone else.
I Love It!

Will the women please stand up!

HOW MANY TIMES have you said, "I can't take this anymore!" but accepted it anyway? How often do you beat up on yourself, criticize yourself, belittle yourself, only to portray to the world how confident, poised, and able you are. Are you thinking no when you say yes? Do you go when you want to stay home? Have you given up when you wanted to push forward? Have you pushed forward when you felt like giving up? Do you ask for it, then doubt you will get it? Have you doubted you would get it, but asked for it anyway? If you have done any of this or any reasonable facsimile thereof, face it, you are confused.

How can we expect life to bless and support when we say one thing, think something else, and feel a completely different way. We are sending the universe mixed messages. The Bible tells us that from one's heart flow the issues of life. The mind and emotions create the "heart" of which the Bible speaks. If our thoughts are confused, our emotions full of doubt, and our action contradictory to our thoughts and emotions, just what do we really expect life to bring us?

In order to get what we want, we must say what we mean. In order to say what we mean, we must know what we want. When we know what we want, we can think and speak positively with great expectations.

Let me be clear.

WHATEVER YOU EXPERIENCE, whatever happens to you is merely a reflection of your need for an attitude adjustment. You can see life as a series of harsh, cruel events that push you too hard and fast; or you can see life as a process of growth and change to which you must adjust. You can see people as vicious, manipulating cutthroats; or you can see them as frightened children, searching to find their way. You can see problems as things you must fight against or struggle with; or you can see them as opportunities which pave new paths. You can see yourself as a hopeless, helpless, defenseless victim; or you can see yourself as a diamond in the rough in the process of transformation. What you see determines what you experience. What you experience is a reflection of what you need to learn. What you need to learn will show up in your life as an experience providing you with an opportunity to demonstrate a new attitude.

I Am having my attitude adjusted!

JUST DO WHAT you do and do it well. Stop worrying about what other people are doing, or what they will say about what you are doing. Just do what you do to the best of your ability. You may never get an award or public recognition or five minutes on the evening news. Just do what you do because you love to do it. Some people may not like what you do or support what you do. But some people will like it and support it, and some will pay you to do it. Whether people like or agree with what you do is not the issue. The issue has to do with what you do; just because you do it can make all the difference in the world.

I have something important to do.

WOULD YOU LIKE to know why you have not found your true purpose in life? The answer is probably in the bottom or the top of your closet. Would you like to know why you never seem to have the money to do all the things you want to do to make your life all that you want it to be? The answer is probably in your dresser drawer—you know, the one with all the junk in it. Do you really want to know why you can never seem to get anywhere on time? The answer is probably down in the basement or in the attic or in the trunk of your car. The reason you can't find the answers is because you do not have order in your life.

Order is the first law of nature. Everything in life happens in an orderly manner. Things must be in place so that when the hand of nature sweeps by it has everything it needs to leave what must be left. When your life and affairs are not in order, nature has no place to put the blessing. And even if the blessing were to be given to you, you probably wouldn't be able to find it. You must bring what you have into total and complete order before you can receive anything else. Order in the secret places! Order in the hidden places! Order in the open places! When you order your visible life, you order your mind. A well-ordered mind is fertile ground for the blessings of Spirit.

Order your life to make way for Spirit.

EVERYONE NEEDS A spiritual discipleship, just like the twelve men who followed the teachings of Christ. A discipleship brings clarity of thought. When you embrace a spiritual discipleship, you are focused and fully committed to a principle greater than yourself. As a spiritual disciple, you have something to believe in, something to work toward, something greater, more beneficial than problems to occupy your mind.

A spiritual disciple must study every aspect of principle and act upon it at all times. When people or circumstances challenge a spiritual disciple, they become the living embodiment of the principle, calling into action the energy to bring balance, harmony, and peace to the situation.

If you are ready to step over obstacles and move through challenges with grace and insight, you are ready to be a spiritual disciple. You will need a brown paper bag and twelve separate slips of paper. On each slip of paper, write one spiritual principle. You may want to choose from among love, faith, truth, acceptance, awareness, understanding, clarity, order, peace, balance, harmony, surrender, discipline, and courage. Drop the slips in the bag. Say a prayer asking for divine guidance and assurance to select the divine principle for you. Reach in and pull out a slip. For the next ninety days, study, meditate upon, and live the energy of the principle. Be that principle in action.

I Am a disciple of _____.

* ✦ * I WONDER WHAT would happen if you stopped worrying about your situation and prayed for somebody else. I know it seems like this is the worst time of your life; you are in pain, totally confused, and you don't know which way to turn. But perhaps if you turned away from the problem for just a minute you might have a breakthrough.

Try it. Close your eyes and pray for someone you know who is sick. Or maybe pray for someone who is homeless, jobless, helplessly locked in an addiction. Pray for someone, perhaps a mother in a war-torn country who does not know where her child, husband, or mother is. What about a mother with a sick child or one who has just buried her child? Pray for a family that is in turmoil; or a child who is lost, in trouble, or both. Pray that your mate will be strong in your times of weakness. Pray for your children, that they will be protected while you are going through this bout of temporary insanity.

I don't know what will happen to your problems while you are praying, but I do know that what you give you get . . . tenfold.

A prayer for somebody is an answered one for me!

MONEY WILL NOT ease the pain we experience in life. It may look that way; it may feel that way; but it is simply not true. Money is *My Own Natural Energy Yield*, a reflection of what I think, feel, and do. It is the manifestation of our beliefs, emotions, and dominant thought patterns. When we believe we are in pain because of the lack of money, or if we engage in a pattern of restrictive thinking, money will not help or save us. It is belief in pain and lack that keeps money from coming to us.

When our purpose in life is to be whole, peace-filled, and loving, we generate positive energy. When we think about how good life is, how blessed we are, how far we have come, we realize we are not restricted. When we seek to give rather than get; when we focus on "do" instead of "cannot do"; when we move beyond pain, fear, doubt, and distress, we open ourselves to a wide range of possibilities. In most cases it is possible to get everything we need and want, with or without money. In all cases, as long as we remain desperate about not having money, the money we seek cannot get to us.

I Am the soul source of my wealth!

Rev. Willie Wilson of Union Temple Church in Washington, D.C., told his congregation to be "planted," not "potted." Potted plants can be knocked over or turned over and easily uprooted. It is very easy for a strong wind or a careless movement to demolish or destroy a potted plant. Potted plants may be beautiful to look at, but they are fragile. They require intensive care, and they die easily under adverse conditions.

Things which are planted have strong roots. They are usually outdoors and able to withstand the winds and the storms. When something is planted, it makes the best of adverse conditions, by grabbing on to whatever is available, to the ground itself, until things get better. When something is planted, it may be nibbled on by varmints; it may be stepped on by the careless; it will be pushed and prodded, but never uprooted. Planting requires reliance on God. Potting is subject to the whims of humans.

I Am planted, not potted.

THOSE THINGS THAT are going to tempt you off the path of your spiritual growth are not going to come up to your front door and ring the bell. Temptations come in through the cracks. They slide under the door! They sneak in through the windows! If you are not careful and always alert, you will be tempted to go right back to your old way of thinking, doing, and being.

Keep the cracks of your heart covered with constant prayer. Ask for divine wisdom and spiritual insight in the midst of all experiences. Seal up the windows of your mind with song. Songs of goodness, songs of praise, and songs that will keep you protected by the watchful eye and guiding ear of the Holy Spirit. Secure the door of your soul with the knowledge of who you are. You are a daughter of light, a woman of power, a child of the Omnipresence of God. Temptation may ring your doorbell, but if you are singing and praying loud enough, you won't even hear it!

Pray a prayer of wisdom! Sing a song of praise!

FINDING THE WAY to joy, peace, abundance, health, and balance requires an examination and evaluation of everything you cherish. In the midst of your evaluation, the Holy Spirit will step in and separate that which is false from that which is true; that which is necessary from that which no longer serves any purpose in your life.

Separation from that which is familiar and cherished is frightening. Yet the Holy Spirit is a spirit of light which will reveal the darkness of the things you have held on to. When the darkness is revealed, what you once cherished will look different! In some cases it will *act* different! The truth is, nothing is different. In the process of evaluation, the presence of the Holy Spirit gives you the ability to see things in a new light. Hopefully that light will set you free.

Everything looks different in the light of Spirit.

The Valley of Nonresistance

Teaches us to cooperate with the flow of life and life's events by surrendering control, the demand to have things our way.

Life is not promised to you. Nor is it promised that it will go the way you want it to, when you want it to.

—ROSALIND CASH

THE OLD SPIRITUAL reminds us, "Nobody told me that the road would be easy . . ." and it's not! It is not easy to shift out of what we do and how we do it. It is not easy to shift our views in order to see new things in place of the old. It is often confusing and frightening to make a shift away from the familiar in order to embrace the unknown. Yet it is a necessary labor we must undertake in order to grow. No matter how difficult, challenging, or hard it may seem, shifts are necessary when the time comes to free ourselves from the confinement of mental, emotional, or physical boxes.

All shifts create a vibration which in turn affects everything around it. If you shift one crayon in a box, all the other crayons will move. Sometimes moving one crayon will cause a slight shift. Under other circumstances, moving one may mean the others fall, crack, and crumble. This is frightening. Sometimes, in fear of the effects our changes will create, we delay making a much-needed shift in our minds and behaviors. As a result, our lives and everything around us remain stuck. When the time comes to move, we must move. The longer we fight against it, the harder and more painful the movement becomes. There is a good thing about life and human nature that we often forget: life and the humans in it move like machinery. When you change gears, everything connected changes too! That is not necessarily a bad thing.

It's time to shift gears.

DEAR GOD,

Into the temple of Your peace I enter to meet You; to share sacred moments in Your presence. In the sanctuary of Your presence I find the peace which heals, which strengthens; the peace which surpasses understanding. Into the womb of Your love, Dear God, I enter, so that You might nourish, protect, and embrace me, for I am Your child. In the shrine of Your abundance I rest my head, wash my hands, cover myself so that You may provide for me all that I need to glorify all that You are.

Into Your home, Dear God, I come once again, to be fed and to rest from the noise of the world. For it is in the sanctuary of Your temple, my heart, that I find You and love You, and understand how much You love me.

Thank You, God
Me

Come unto me all you that labor, and I will give you rest.

⚡ YOLANDA ADAMS SINGS a song that reminds us, "The battle is not yours . . . it's the Lord's!" I love that song because it reminds us that we are not required by life or in life to fight with people or conditions. The only thing required of us is to faithfully trust in the omnipresence of the all-knowing Creator to handle every situation according to Divine Law. Make no mistake, that in and of itself is a challenging task. It is quite difficult to be under pressure, under attack, by people you can see or tangible life experiences, and to remember that God is always in charge. It takes a very powerful person not to get sucked into the appearance of disaster or the onslaught of trouble. It takes strength and nerves of steel not to answer false accusations, not to defend oneself against seeming injustices, because to the human psyche, not to do anything is to be passive. Nothing could be further from the truth.

It's not my battle!

WHEN WE REFUSE to surrender our power when we are attacked or when we encounter trouble, we are exercising the knowledge of our authentic power. There is an old gospel song that reminds us, "No matter what you are going through, remember God is using you." God is our power, the source of our strength and our good. When we face difficulties, God will use the opportunity to demonstrate just how powerful S/He is. When we do nothing, we are doing the best thing. We are actually providing the Creator with the opportunity to do everything, according to His/Her will. It is not the Creator's will that we suffer, struggle, fight, or die in the battle to save ourselves from life. God will fight the battles on our behalf when we move out of the way. The challenge is to realize that the movement required is no movement, no word, no fight. To be in trusting, faithful stillness is to be in God's powerful armor.

To do nothing is to do something with God!

ARE YOU PUSHING, struggling, trying to get something done, but getting nowhere? When it seems that nothing you are doing is making anything any better, it is time to call on Divine Mind. Divine Mind is the strength, the power, the ever-present, all-knowing energy of life within you. Divine Mind can do what you could never imagine doing. But first, you must stop doing and allow Divine Mind to work.

Divine Mind can move the mountain, part the sea, stop the turmoil. It can straighten that man right up, bring that child back into the fold, move that supervisor to another location, or find some money in the budget. Divine Mind is able to dissolve that tumor, cleanse the immune system, lower the blood pressure or the amount of sugar in the bloodstream. Only Divine Mind can destroy the dependency on drugs or food or alcohol, or eliminate any bad habit, thought, or emotion.

Now if you are truly ready to put an end to suffering, move around the obstacles, get rid of the pain, find a way out of "no way" and save yourself some grief, here's what you have to do. Give up the need to be right! Stop demanding that things go your way! Stop talking about what you don't want! Don't have! Can't do! Speak your good into existence with power, dominion, and authority! Move your limited human-self out of the way and watch Divine Mind work for you.

Divine Mind is always mine!

THE RENT IS due, and you have no cash on hand. You are hopelessly, desperately, foolishly in love, and he doesn't know your name. You have lost some important papers at work, and your supervisor is asking for them. You cleverly embellished your expenses for the year, and now the IRS is auditing you. You squeezed that new pair of shoes onto your charge account, and now the bill is due, along with the rent. What do you do? NOTHING!

No matter what is going on in your life, the planets are still moving around the sun. Seeds are turning into flowers. Embryos are turning into babies. The moon is becoming full. The sun is rising. Things are going to happen, and you have a choice: you can be a witness or a participant. A witness observes and learns. A participant creates drama and stress.

No matter what it looks like, the truth is simple: there is something you are learning or unlearning. There is some part of you that must be refined. Not fixed! Not changed! But fine-tuned in order to operate at a higher level of efficiency. You may not like what is going on, but you will live through it, if you give up the need to fix it. Surrender control with a deep breath. Forgive yourself for any poor choices. Make a commitment to work on your weak areas. Trust yourself to know that you will know exactly what to do when the time comes to do it. In the meantime, go pick a flower, hug a baby, or salute the sun.

Only good can come out of this.

My grandma always said, "Trouble is what God uses to prepare you for better things!"

If you have trouble in your life, you are in a valley. If you are in a valley, you are being prepared for something bigger, better, greater; something you probably could not handle now.

Trouble has a way of sharpening underutilized skills such as patience, trust, and spiritual insight. Trouble disciplines the mind. When you have trouble in your life, you are forced to focus on what you must do. The best kind of trouble is the kind that strengthens the character by showing you that you really can do the very thing you convinced yourself you could not do. Most of all, trouble builds your faith. In your moment of greatest need, you have to have faith that you will be all right.

When your life is not working out the way you want it to work, faithful trust and patience lead to new insights about the power of God. If you can remember not to panic but to trust; not to get busy but to be still; not to whine or complain but to praise, you will undoubtedly remember how merciful God is. This insight will prove to be valuable, whether you are in trouble or not.

I Am being prepared for my greater good!

WHEN MY MOTHER died, I learned the value of independence. When I was raped, I learned that I was so much more than a body. When my father died, I learned about forgiveness. In an abusive marriage, I learned self-value and self-worth. Of course, I did not realize I was learning until long after the experience and the lesson were over.

Every experience, no matter how painful, traumatic, unexpected, or confusing it may seem, is an opportunity to learn. At times, we learn about our selves. In other instances, we learn about others. We learn what to do, what not to do. We learn when to wait, how long we are capable of waiting. In the midst of the most difficult lesson, we learn the tenacity of spirit and how far it will take us. At the end of it all, we have developed character.

Always remember, every experience is merely a trip through life's classroom. Some classes have big, fat, ugly, mean teachers; this does not mean they do not know what they are doing. In some classes, you will have a great deal of homework. Good! You are being forced to study, pay attention, and take copious notes. In each of life's learning experiences, our job is to get the lesson, and practice what we have learned. What will make the lessons easier is to remember, everything you learn can someday be put to good use, and you will be better because of what you have learned.

I Am a student of life!

223

ONE OF THE good things about valley experiences is that they remind us to take off our Superwoman capes for just a while. It doesn't mean we can't put the cape back on. It simply means we recognize the need to rest, to stop, to be still. Valleys remind us we can't do work, the kids, his crisis, their issues, Momma, and ourselves. Since so many of us have a problem saying no, life devises clever little ways to help us say it. Perhaps that is exactly where you are now.

Think of it this way: if you had a broken leg, you would not try to run a marathon. If you had a cold, you would not walk in the rain. Yet when we are tired, confused, overwhelmed, or just plain old fed up, we often do not know how to stop. We fly around doing and giving and trying. Being in the valley is like having a big hole in your cape. You can't fly. You are grounded. You are forced to go within.

Do not resist this blessed opportunity to mend your mind, body, or spirit. Put the shades down. Close the blinds. Turn off the motor. Shake your cape out, cover your body with it, lay down, and take a nap. Everything you think you must do today will be there tomorrow. You can handle it then, when you are rested, clear, and stronger. Anything that can't wait, won't wait, and it will not be there for you to handle.

Just a minute, please!
_____

TAKE A MOMENT to step back and watch the sun rise or set. If you can be still long enough to observe the process, you will realize it is the earth, not the sun, that is moving. What a wonderful revelation! The world is in a constant state of motion. Some things are moving, changing, turning, dying, and being born, while other things are constant. Once you realize this, you will know that (1) wherever you were yesterday you are not today and (2) whatever you are today you will not be tomorrow. Whoever you will be tomorrow you cannot be today. Whatever you know today will look different than it did yesterday. And what you don't know today, you will know tomorrow. After all, the world is in the process of being made, and so are you. Be still. Watch the process. Learn from what you see. Practice what you know. And then, watch how it all changes.

Wait a minute, let me change!

NINETY PERCENT OF what you are cannot be seen with the physical eye. You cannot see what happened to you yesterday, last week, or two years ago. You cannot see what you will be in two days, two weeks, or two months. No one can see your thoughts or your feelings. Even you can't see your own anger, fear, guilt, or shame. You cannot see most of the things you worry and fret about, and they take up so much of your time and energy that you cannot see how wonderful you are right now!

One of the things that you cannot see is the powerful energy around you. It is an awesome energy that protects and guides you. It is an energy that holds you up, lights you up, and picks you up when you fall down. It is the energy of the *Mother.* You can't see Her so you ignore Her. Like the problems and the past you worry about, the *Mother* cannot be detected with the naked eye. Because She cannot be seen, you doubt that She is real. This seems to make perfectly good sense, since seeing is believing. If that is so, why do you give so much attention to other invisible things that can never do for you what the *Mother* has already done?

Don't ignore your Mother!

CAN WE JUST be blessed right now? Can we find something, some one thing to be happy about, satisfied with, excited over? It won't cost us anything to smile and pat ourselves on the back for what we have already done and overcome. If we really understood that right where we are is exactly where we need be, we would find the joy we convince ourselves we are missing.

Life is so much smarter than we are, it never moves too quickly, nor does it skip any steps. Life always shows up on time and in time to bless, teach, reward, heal, protect, or guide us. Life always knows exactly what we need, what we are ready for, and when we are prepared to receive it. We are usually so busy looking behind or ahead, we miss the flow of life passing right before our eyes. Fear, anxiety, guilt, and shame fog our vision and cause us to miss the point, the lesson, and the blessings that are present right now. Let us remember that right now is a blessing. When we understand that, we stop second-guessing life.

In the presence of now, I Am.

ARE YOU TIRED? Fed Up? Messed up in mind or body? Have you given your all, all for nothing? Do you feel abused, abandoned, generally on the downhill side of life? Well, have I got something for you! Call 1-800-SPIRIT for instant relief from the load of your life.

No other product on the market or person in the world can provide faster relief than SPIRIT.

1-800-SPIRIT is the way to permanent resolution of those pesky problems, paralyzing fears, re-occurring bouts with self-doubt and self-defeat. 1-800-SPIRIT is the key if you've tried everything else and none of it worked!

Put an end to panic!

Remove unwanted conditions and people!

Stop the merry-go-round of 2 steps up and 10 steps back!

Don't delay! Call today! 1-800-SPIRIT!

Operators are on duty 24 hours a day! 1-800-SPIRIT!

Do It NOW!

Hello, 1-800-SPIRIT—I've got a problem!

THE TRUTH OF the matter is, we cannot expect to be in control of the circumstances in our lives when we cannot control our minds for five minutes. We can spend years running around in an attempt to make certain that things happen or don't happen before we realize that nothing is getting done. While we have so much to do, we resist and in some cases refuse to spend five minutes a day trying to reach the Master Repairman, the one who is truly in control of our lives. The only one who can fix us when we are broken.

Meditation is more than doing nothing. It is the art of listening. It is a practice which enables us to tune in and fine-tune the key areas of our lives: the mind and the spirit. Meditation is the daily minimum requirement that will prevent us from breaking down and falling apart—at the most inopportune moments. Some of us are so afraid of losing control, we can convince ourselves we don't know how to meditate; we don't have time to meditate; or even if we stop to meditate, the problem will still exist when the meditation is over. These are all clever little excuses to ensure that we stay in control of things we can't control. If you are one of us who uses one of these excuses, ask yourself, what method would you suggest to give the Repairman time to work?

I believe it is time for some repair work!

THE MIND IS such a wonderful and divine instrument, it knows exactly when we need protection. In such cases, the mind will give us an excuse or rationale we can grab onto to shield us from harmful, hurtful situations. These "defense mechanisms" the mind offers us are but a temporary shelter in the midst of a raging storm. It is our duty, however, to move from beneath this shelter when it no longer serves our highest or greatest good. In other words, when it keeps us from growing.

Be sure not to tell yourself you "don't" when you do want it. Be mindful not to accept "you can't" when you know you can. Pay attention to the excuses you make not to, when you know you must. Don't settle for less when you desire more. No matter how hard you think it is, ask for what you need and what you want when you need it or want it. Pay attention to the inner chatter which will take a temporary defense mechanism and turn it into a crutch.

I will not excuse away my truth.

SPIRIT NEVER FAILS. While it may seem as if you can call out and get no answer, spirit never fails to answer a sincere call. We will call a friend ten or twenty times until we get an answer. Yet we call out to spirit once and only half expect an answer. Unfortunately, many of our calls to spirit are filled with doubt, fear, unreasonable demands, and unworthy requests. These calls will receive a busy signal. Only when we open our hearts, bring forth the pure unadulterated truth, and rely on spirit to show up, will we receive the divine response, in the divine way, in the divine time. Spirit never fails! We, however, often fail to make the proper connections.

I have a spiritual connection!

WHAT DO YOU do when you just can't shake "feel bad"? You keep telling yourself you shouldn't, because you've got so much to be grateful for. You try to smile, to laugh, to talk yourself into a better mood, but nothing works. What do you do when, for no apparent reason, you feel sad or angry or downright ugly? You find yourself snapping at people. Perhaps you feel like crying. In the back of your mind, there is a feeling of hopelessness. In the pit of your stomach, there is a feeling of helplessness. You can't talk. You don't want to be bothered. What do you do? Allow yourself to feel it!

Do not be afraid to experience your emotions; they are the path to your soul. Emotions erupt to remind us we are alive, that we are human. And to let us know we are growing. Trust yourself enough to feel what you feel. If you feel like crying—cry. If you want to scream— scream. Get right down into the pit of helplessness and hopelessness. Allow the fear to have its way with you. Stay with yourself. Be in yourself. Ride it out when you feel bad; honor it, and know, once it's over, it's over . . . until the next time.

The worse I feel, the better I get!

IT'S NOT THE problem, the people, or the situation. It is your resistance to the problem, the people, or the situation which causes pain, anger, fear, or frustration. Resistance is when an immovable force encounters an unrelenting energy. Something comes at you. You don't want to know it, see it, or hear about it. Maybe you want to be right. Could it be that you are trying to get your way, and someone or something is in the way? Perhaps you are afraid and don't want to admit it, and now something or someone is challenging you. What do you do? You could cooperate.

When resistance comes up in your body, you want to shut down or run away. It may feel like you just don't want to be bothered. Unfortunately, if you shut down, you will miss a valuable growth experience and an opportunity to get in touch with yourself. Cooperation means you do not try to block the energy, within you or in the environment. Listening to what is being said does not mean that you have to act. Allow yourself to feel it and decide what to do about it later. Make a decision. Take a risk. Whatever comes at you is coming to teach you or heal you. Whatever you do, don't push the experience away. If you do, it will show up later with more force and urgency.

I Am open to this experience.

YOU CAN'T DO anything as long as you are afraid of what might happen. Fear makes the problem seem so much bigger than it may be. Fear freezes the mind, making the challenge seem overwhelming. Fear clouds opportunities, erases possibilities, and limits the ability to move beyond the place in which the mind is stuck. Unfortunately, we don't always realize we are afraid. We may think we are protecting ourselves or taking a positive stance against a negative influence. Fear also makes us delusionary.

A friend of mine became extremely ill, but would not go to the doctor. She continued to work, having convinced herself she could beat whatever it was. She admitted she was afraid to hear what the doctor might say. She did not want to hear it. I prayed with her and convinced her she had to have a name, an idea of what the problem was. She did not have to claim it or believe it, but she had to know what she was up against. Without the name and the knowledge, fear, not the condition, was her enemy.

No matter how difficult we think the problem is, we must muster up the courage to face it. Very often we find that what we think is the matter, is not the matter at all. Fear, however, is a matter we must be willing to confront, stare down, and move around. Fear can make a small matter appear disproportionately greater than our ability. However, we have the ability to put fear in its right place, a place where we do not have to be.

I want to hear all the facts.

The Valley of Success

*Teaches us how to ask for what we want
and expect to get it, even when it makes
others unhappy.*

It's about believin' when you ain't got nothin' to believe in.

—WHITNEY HOUSTON

DEAR GOD,

There are so many good things I want, but for some reason I am afraid to ask You for them. Maybe it's because I was denied so much as a child. Or it could be that so much of the happiness I have known was closely followed by pain. I don't know why I don't ask for my good, and I don't have to know. What I do know is, God, I am ready to be healed of this affliction. I am ready to receive all the good You have in store for me because I know that what You want me to have is probably more than I would ask for anyway.

So, go ahead and bless me, God; shower Your good on me so abundantly that I won't have time to protest or get in the way. Bless me right now, God, with all the good You know I can possibly manage. Shut my mouth with good. Open my heart with good. Clear my mind with good. Order my life to receive Your abundant good, in the most divine ways imaginable. Go ahead God, bless me. I dare You! After all, You know what I need before I ask. Go ahead! Make my day! Bless me! Thank You, God.

I am ready to be blessed!

EVEN ON THE spiritual path, things are not always going to be rosy. There will be difficult situations and people, bad days and hard times all along the way. You have moments, days, sometimes weeks when you will doubt yourself, and there will be times when you doubt the power of spirit. You may get sick. You may feel inadequate. You may lose things or people you hold dear. Just know, it is all part of the process.

For some reason, we think that spirit will miraculously change everything for the better. Eventually it may; however, the search for spirit, the quest for truth, the desire for peace usually rips the foundation of our lives apart. There are thoughts, feelings, habits, and conditions we have embraced which are grounded in fear, anger, judgment, and ego. The farther we move along the path toward a more spiritual life, the more we must be willing to release. Our trying times and major challenges are a process of release.

Things must come up in order to move out.

YOUR LIFE HAS always been a process of growing and outgrowing. You quickly outgrew your clothes as an infant. You outgrew your shoes before you wore them out. You took great pride when you grew beyond that mark on the tree, the door frame, or the chart in school. You were happy when you grew through puberty into your adolescent body. However, for some reason, today it is difficult to accept you have outgrown a habit, career, relationship, or even your hometown. You hold on, afraid to let go, trying to make it work, subjecting yourself to physical, emotional, and spiritual pain. This is not a good thing!

If life is going to work in your behalf, you must give yourself permission to grow. If it no longer makes you happy; if you are searching unsuccessfully for ways to make it work; if you know in your heart of hearts that whatever it is, it's over—let go and grow. Be willing to search for new ways to grow. Be open to new environments to grow in. Always be on the lookout for people who are growing and are willing to help you grow. Never feel bad about your growth. Some people will not support you. Others will try to make you feel bad. You might be afraid. You might even experience some pain. Know that it is all a part of growing and growing up. If you need a little taste of the pain you will create when you do not allow yourself to grow, stick your feet in the shoes you wore to the high school prom.

I accept life's challenge to grow!

KEEPING WHAT YOU have, even when it does not make you happy, leaves no room for your good to get in. Holding on to what is old, worn-out, or unproductive, because you cannot see your good coming, delays it from breaking through to you. As hard as it may be, and as frightened as you may be, you must let go of all you don't want in order to get all that you want.

The universe does not tolerate a void where there is a need. It will fill all empty spaces with its divine substance. When you have a request and make it known, the universe gladly responds. There is more than enough of everything to go around to everyone. However, it is up to you to make space in your life and be ready to receive what you want.

You can always have what you want, exactly the way you want it. There is never a good reason to compromise or settle for less. You can have as much as you can stand, of whatever it is you want, as soon as you are ready to receive it. You can have it now, right where you are, exactly as you are. You do not have to be perfected in order to be blessed. In order for any of this to happen, remember you must fulfill one small requirement; you must say, "NO!" to what you don't want in order to make room for what you want.

I Am open, ready, and willing to receive.

IN HER BOOK on relationships, Sonya Ray wrote, "God is the affirmative energy behind every idea and thought we have." In essence, God always says yes to our thoughts. If we think positive thoughts about our self and life, God says yes to us. If we harbor negative thoughts or damaging ideas, God does not censor us. The affirmative energy of God supports us in our self-proclaimed downfall.

Knowing that you have the power of the universe, the power of God in your corner and on your side, should make you feel better. The Bible says, "The Lord Almighty is your husband." In effect this makes each of us Mrs. Almighty! We are fully equipped, perfectly capable of facing any situation, under any circumstances, and coming out on top. The key is thinking we can, knowing we will, believing with all our hearts that all is well, no matter what it looks like. If you think it, God will always say yes to you.

When I say yes, God affirms it!

IF GOD WERE to tell you that all of your problems would be solved if you did one thing, would you be willing to do it? No matter what it was? Imagine, we are talking about God, the Creator, the Giver, the Keeper of Life. God, who has the power to do all things and is giving you a verbal guarantee that if you willingly undertake one task, all the success, health, wealth, joy, peace, and love you can stand would be yours. What would you say? Throughout the next few pages, let us explore some possible responses and reactions we might have to such a challenge. We will begin with the instructions from God.

Okay, God, I'm ready!

MY DEAR CHILD,

I have heard your many pleas for My help. You have asked what you should do to improve your life. You have asked why things never go your way. I smile when you ask these things because everything in your life is just the way you want it. You are so powerful, you are creating every second of every minute within the day. You have had your way, but you are not happy with the way it looks. I am pleased that you have finally agreed to try My way.

There is unlimited abundance, total well-being, and peace beyond understanding for the rest of your life waiting for you at the end of this task. All I ask of you is that you climb the highest mountain, one step at a time, one day at a time. I assure you I will be with you every step of the way. You may bring whatever you like. It is up to you to figure out what you will need, what you will eat, and what you will wear. You can choose to travel alone or to bring a companion. You can begin the journey whenever you like. The only requirement I give you is, take one step every day, until you reach the top. I will be awaiting your arrival.

Be Blessed, My Beloved,
I Am

Come unto me all who labor. I will give you rest.

———

DEAR GOD,

I really want to take the journey up the mountain, but I don't think it's fair that I can only take one step a day. That would take forever! Why can't I walk until I am tired? Why can't I take a helicopter part of the way and walk the rest? And You know what else, God? I've never been up a mountain in all my life! I have no idea what to bring! Is it cold up there? Do I need boots or sneakers? I've heard that the air is very thin in the mountains. Does that mean I should bring oxygen? How much should I bring? Besides that, how am I supposed to carry oxygen tanks with all the other gear I'll need? I need pots, pans, clothes, books, water, my radio, and a tent. I really think You are asking too much!

Now, I know You are God and everything, but there could be wild animals along the way. Don't You think I'll need a gun or a knife or something? But then You say, "Thou shall not kill." So I was wondering, how do You expect me to protect myself? Sure, You'll be with me, but the bears aren't going to eat You, are they? Don't get me wrong, I really would like to come up the mountain. I have been waiting to have all the things You promised. But I just don't think I can do it. Besides that, how would I get down?

Love,
Me

The will makes the way!

DEAR GOD,

I was all ready to start my trip up the mountain, but my sister messed me up. She wanted to come with me, but she has two kids. I told her we would find someone to keep them, and we did. But she didn't have the money to pay them, so I did. But then her boyfriend came home. She didn't want him to know anything about what we were doing (You know how he is), so she said we had to wait until he went back down South. That guy stayed here for two weeks! He's not working or anything. I lent her some money for food. I kept the kids three days so they could, well, You know. Then they had this big fight over at my mother's house, and I told her she was a fool, so she stopped speaking to me. She always does that.

After he left, she didn't speak to me for two more weeks. Yesterday she called and said she's ready to go. Now I don't have any money to buy the things I need. So I guess I'll have to wait until next year when I get my next bonus check.

I Am,
Helpful!

Help yourself first!

DEAR GOD,

I was on my way to the mountaintop, taking one step a day, just like You said. One day, after I had stopped, I met this really nice guy. I have no idea what he was doing way up there, but he said he needed a place to stay. It was freezing that day, so I couldn't leave him outside. I invited him in. Well, we got to talking, and he really was very nice. The next morning, I got up, fixed his breakfast, and packed up so that we could move forward. He slept until 4 o'clock! By the time he got up, washed up, shaved, and ate, it was 6:30 and very dark. He promised to get up early the next day so we could take the next step together.

I can't lie to You, God, he wore me out that night! So the next day, I overslept. To make a long story short, this went on for three weeks. We stayed in the same place without moving forward. It was fun, but I finally had to put my foot down. The next morning, he told me that he couldn't go with me because he didn't have any gear. He said he would go down and get some and meet me in a week. That was a month ago. Now I have no food, and he took my hiking boots. Before I can continue, I have to go all the way down to the bottom, restock my supplies, and start all over again. Hopefully I'll see You soon.

Just a step away,
I Am

Ain't gonna let nobody turn me around!

DEAR GOD,

You will never believe what happened to me about the mountaintop thing. When I heard what You said, I called my best friend right away. We always share good news. At first, she didn't believe me. I kept trying to convince her, but she said I was crazy. Then one day her other girlfriend from down the street told her the same thing; then she believed it, so we all decided we would go together. We had a planning meeting to decide who would bring what. Sixteen people showed up for the meeting. Some of them didn't even know why they had come. By the time we explained everything, elected officers, established committees, and collected dues, it was too late to discuss travel plans. We set the next meeting for a week later.

Only eight people showed up for the next meeting, and the treasurer didn't come. Twelve people showed up for the next meeting, but the new treasurer didn't come. This week only ten people showed up, but the head of the food committee, the safety committee, and the gear committee said they couldn't go. I told them I was leaving in two weeks, with or without them. This morning I got two postcards. The first treasurer is at the top of the mountain! The second treasurer is about half way up! I'm not coming! I refuse to spend time on the same mountain with those people!

Unbelievably Yours,

I Am

Fewness of words make greatness of deeds.

————

DEAR GOD,

How do You expect me to climb a mountain to find my good? You know I broke my leg back in '56, and my knee has been messed up since then. Sure I play tennis, but that's therapy. I do it because I have to. And what about my blood pressure? You know I'm on a special diet. I can't eat out of cans, and I can't eat char-broiled food. They give me gas. Besides that, how can I soak my feet on a mountain plateau? You know I have arthritis, and the cold just makes it worse.

I've worked hard all my life. I've raised my kids, and I help them out with my grandkids. How do You expect me to leave them? Suppose they need me? And who is going to get my retirement check if I'm not here? What will I do for money up there? And You know I have to watch the soaps! I'm too old and tired to do this, and I don't think it's fair that You are making it so hard on people like me. I sincerely hope You will reconsider Your requirements and make special accommodations for the folks like me who have special needs.

Sincerely,
Worn out,
I Am

Age ain't nothin' but a number.

MY DEAREST FATHER,

I would like to thank You for this opportunity. This is an answer to my prayers. As You know, I have been homeless for a year now. This is a chance for me to do something useful with my time. Whether I make it or not doesn't matter. I am grateful for the opportunity to try. So many days I have waited for meals and leads, so I have learned patience. One step a day is just fine with me. But I do need Your help with a few things.

I own only the clothes on my back and a blanket. God, please let it be warm during my journey. I have no gear and no food. I am trusting You to provide a little something for me to eat along the way. I don't own a map or a flashlight. Please make the path to the top very clear. And if for some reason You cannot do these things I ask You to keep my body strong. I can sleep in the cold and the dark. I can eat leaves or raw meat or go hungry. What I cannot do is live one day without Your strength, Your love, Your breath in my body. I know I will see You soon. I shall not fail, and I will not falter with Your help. Please keep an eye on me, God, and know whatever good I find at the top of the mountain, I will use to help others.

Truly blessed,
I Am

All that the Father has is mine.

MY DEAR CHILD,

Always remember I love you. I created you out of Myself; how can I abandon you? When I love you, I am loving Myself. I Am the Spirit of life within you. I can never take Myself away from you.

You look everywhere to everyone before you come to Me. You grab hold of things and push Me away for them. I Am your good, your source, and your supply. Whatever you choose for yourself, I will always say yes. Whatever you do with your life, I will always be there. Whatever you want for yourself, I have more than enough to give you and keep you forever.

In the midst of fear, seek My strength. In the midst of confusion, choose My peace. When your trials and burdens overwhelm you, give them to Me. I always know what to do to restore order and balance to Myself.

> The Joy of the World,
> I Am

God is the good in me.

PERHAPS YOU WENT to bed last night thinking about the overdue bills, the lack of finances, the problematic people and situations you have to face. This morning you woke up. Did you give thanks? Maybe your back is out; your leg may be broken; your head is stopped up, or your eye is swollen. So you are in pain, in fear, in an uncomfortable state, but did you give thanks? You may be alone, heartbroken, confused, or disappointed, but the issue still remains, did you give thanks?

Let's put it this way: you can think, you can feel, you are alive. You've got a brain, a life, an idea. All of this means that someway, someday, you can do better. So . . . did you give thanks? If you didn't, it is probably because you forgot that when the praise goes up, the blessings come down. That should be enough to inspire you to be thankful.

What a blessing! I am so thankful!

THERE IS A song sung by Darryl Coley in which he states, "He is preparing me for things I cannot handle now." That's exactly what life's tests and lessons are about: preparation. Once we understand this, we can dispense with the notion that something is wrong with us or that we have done something wrong. Life is not out to prove you wrong. Life made you—right? Just as we are divinely made, we must be divinely prepared.

Think back to the time when you were sixteen, nineteen, or twenty years old. Remember how you were convinced that you knew everything you needed to know. And weren't you always right? Now remember how your mind was changed, your attitude adjusted through various experiences, some good, some not so good. The people you "knew" and thought were so wonderful turned out to be just the opposite. The things you thought you couldn't live without are now scattered memories. Your opinions changed. Your loyalties shifted. Those experiences were preparation and training for who you are and what you do now.

No matter what is going on in your life today, remember, it is only preparation. People roam and go; situations rise and fall; it's all preparation for better things. We must stretch, reach, grow into your goodness. Without the preparation we receive through adversity, disappointment, confusion, or pain, we could not appreciate the goodness when it arrives.

On the other side of this, there is goodness.

DEAR SELF,
DO IT!
Pray!
Meditate!
Exercise!
Stretch!
Take a Risk!
Then,
Pray!
Meditate!
Give Thanks!
Do it! Do it! Do it! Every day.
You'll be a lot better for it.

I Am doing it! I Am doing it! I Am doing it!

ARE YOU A Zebedee? Zebedee was a fisherman who was busy mending his nets when Christ came by. Christ invited Zebedee and his sons James and John to join him in his travels and work. James and John went with Christ and ultimately became disciples. Zebedee stayed behind. He was too busy mending his nets.

How often have you had a good idea pop into your mind, but were too busy to follow it up? How many invitations and opportunities have you passed up because you had too much to do? How many times has your soul cried out to be something, to do something, to have something, but you had too many other things going on? Sounds to me like you could be a Zebedee!

The spirit of life speaks directly into our hearts and minds. When we are disobedient it will speak to us through other people. Questions and suggestions which seem to have little significance, could be the key to your goodness. If you are too busy to listen, you just might miss your place in glory. Take time to listen to yourself. Make time to talk and listen to others. Don't be a Zebedee! Spirit may have some very important work for you to do.

I'm never too busy for Spirit.

HOW BUSY ARE you? Are you so very busy that the quality of your friendships and loveships are beginning to suffer? Are you so busy you don't have time to clean or cook or watch cartoons with the children on Saturday morning? Is your life so filled with action and activity that little details like your sister's anniversary, your daughter's tea party, a leisurely chat with your mother, just slip your mind? Well, if you are that busy, something is definitely out of balance.

The busiest people I know are the most frightened people I know. They are afraid they won't be seen. Afraid they won't be heard. Afraid they won't do enough to be seen and heard. Being busy is like flying—the harder you flap your wings, the farther you go, the more you leave behind. Unfortunately, there are times when what we are flying to is not as loving, supportive, or necessary as what we fly away from. The key is to remember balance.

It is possible to do all the things you want to do while sprinkling it with a few things you need to do. Make a list of every important person and activity in your life. Make a schedule allowing quality time for everything and everyone on your list. Give yourself time or a day you will spend on each project and with each person. People you cannot see, you can call. Things you cannot do, ask others to do them for you. Quality, not quantity, is important in our lives. A little bit of everything will still mean we are busy, but at least we will be doing all that matters.

I Am never too busy to do what counts.

———

DEAR GOD:

Please shut my mouth! I always seem to say things I don't want to say, in places I don't want to say them, to people I don't need to say them to. I have a habit of speaking my dreams aloud before they are ready to be born; my criticisms before I have complete information; my fears, which have no power until I utter them.

Lord, please lock my lips! I no longer want to yell when I'm angry, beat up on myself when I think I am wrong, swear when I'm afraid or talk just because everybody else is talking. This morning I asked myself, "How stupid could you be?" Yesterday I told myself I couldn't do any better. Just last week, I remember having an in-depth conversation with me about all that was wrong with me. My tongue seems to have a mind of its own, and it uses my mouth to create things I have to live down. I know words have power, but my tongue sometimes forgets.

Dear Lord, I give You permission to shut my mouth for at least twenty minutes every day. When I open it again, let it be under Your divine supervision. Let me speak words of forgiveness to myself and others. Let my mouth become a vessel of Your grace and Your love. May the words that I speak bring to life the essence that is You. From this day forward, let the words of my mouth be acceptable to You.

Thank You, God. And so it is!

What would God say in this situation?

———

HOW CAN YOU tell when you are being called upon to be patient and when you are being called upon to take action? There will be those situations when you will be absolutely torn and very confused about what to do. Should you be patient, seemingly passive, or should you defend your rights, your space, or your "Self"? Your heart may say that you are being tested while your ego is screaming, "You can't do that to me!" How can you determine what is the right thing to do? I have discovered that you won't know until you get still.

In all situations you must stop before you move. Not until you stop, look, and listen will you receive divine guidance. Stop worrying. Stop blaming. Stop being angry and outraged. Look at the situation from all angles and sides. Look for your lesson and your share of responsibility. Then, you must turn within and listen for the guidance of Spirit.

If your lesson is to be still or patient, miraculously you will find the strength to let go and know that God's way is always the perfect way. If it is God's will that you should act or speak, something inside your being will stand up, move your feet, and point you in the right direction. When you are patient enough to stop, look, and listen, asking what to do, you will always be shown how to do it.

Stop! Look! Listen before you act!

THE HUMAN PSYCHE is the most fragile possession we have. It doesn't take much to damage, in some cases shatter, our sense of self and security within our being. Most of the damage occurs between our birth and the age of five. The things we see, hear, and experience in our childhood create or destroy the foundation of self which we carry throughout our lives.

Because we have little conscious memory of what happened in our earliest days, many of us walk through life with a nagging, dull ache in our minds; a sense of worthlessness, valuelessness, hopelessness we just cannot seem to shake. It may show up as unfulfilling work, broken relationships, obesity, unexplained fears and apprehensions. We find ourselves on a treadmill of despair, and cannot seem to get off.

When you find yourself in a never-ending cycle of despair, do not be afraid or ashamed to seek help: get a therapist, join a support group, go for counseling. Many of us believe it to be a negative commentary about who we are if we admit we need help. Perhaps as children, our voice, our needs, or our cries for help were ignored. As adults, we repeat the pattern of neglect, unknowingly. Therapists, psychologists, psychiatrists are trained to heal the human psyche. That is their job. Your job is to bring them to the part of you they have been trained to heal.

It is okay to ask for help.

YOU BEHAVE DIFFERENTLY when you know someone is watching you. Just as children sit up straight when the teacher is in the classroom or workers exert a little extra effort when the supervisor passes by, it is human nature to do a little more and a little better when you know someone is watching you. Has it occurred to you that someone is always watching you? Have you ever considered that the someone is God?

God is always watching what you do and how you do it. S/He wants to see how you handle your tests and challenges and whether or not you are grateful for your blessings. God is listening to every word you say. How you talk to other people and what you say about other people is very important to God. Your words reveal your knowledge and understanding of the power that you have been given, the power to create and destroy with the words you speak. Most important, God is paying very close attention to how you treat *you* and what you say to *you*. God wants to know if you *act* like you know that *you* are a unique manifestation of God.

Someone is always watching you.

WHO DO YOU think you are?
> *Don't you know you are a child of God?*

What do you want to be?
> *Isn't what you are enough for you? For the world?*

Why do you think you are inadequate? Imperfect?
> *Don't you know you are too powerful to be measured or contained?*

Why are you stumbling around in darkness?
> *Could it be you are afraid of your light?*

Why do you accept mediocrity in your life?
> *Is it just to make others feel good about you?*

What could be better for you than the love of God?
> *Could it be you can't stand to be loved?*

Just who do you really think you are?
> *Why isn't being a powerful light of God's love enough to get you through?*

I Am that I Am.

IF YOU CONTINUE to think of the situation as a problem, it will continue to be a problem. If you continue to think of "that person" or "these people" as your enemy or adversary, they will continue to hound and haunt you. If you continue to say, "I can't," "I don't know how," "They won't let me," you won't, they won't, and it will never get done. If you continue to feel bad, it will only get worse. The truth is, it's your problem and your choice.

Take a moment or a day to feel what you feel, but then regroup. Realize that you are powerful! You have something to say about what happens to you! Then realize that the way a situation affects you, hurts you, frightens you, angers you, disarms you, inspires you, motivates you, transforms you, or empowers you is entirely up to you. Maybe you didn't make it happen to you, but you can certainly decide how to make it happen for you. The issue is, how are you going to deal with it?

I can turn this around for my own good.

___

YOUR LIFE IS your train. You are the conductor and a passenger. How your train moves and where it ends up is totally up to you. Your talents and abilities, dreams and goals are your tickets. Now don't get excited just because you have a ticket. If you do not use it, you won't go anywhere.

Opportunities are stations along the way. If you are not at the station on time, you will be left standing at the station with all the other people who merely have tickets. The train will not wait for you. You cannot hold the train for people who are late. You cannot stop the train at every station to make sure everybody who wants to ride is on the train. Keep your train well fueled, keep it clean, be on the lookout for nicks and cracks in the tracks. Above all else, be sure you don't run over people. Move out at a steady pace, slow but sure. If you are a conscientious and alert conductor, your train will never take a wrong turn.

My train is taking off.

✳ VERY OFTEN, WHEN people upset us or hurt us, it is because there was no agreement. Agreements give clarity. They bring about order and understanding. Agreements are an important element of success. Without an agreement, you can be thinking one thing while the other person has a completely different idea. In the end, you may have both lived up to your agreement; however, there was no clarity on what you were in agreement about.

Agreements are important when we are living together, working together, or trying to get to some place together. Agreements must be clear, and spoken rather than implied. Agreements must be respected. There must be a meeting of the minds which everyone can live with. Agreements must be honored. All who agree must keep their word to do what they say they will do. When there is no agreement, those who are coming together can expect to accomplish only a few things: a lot of confusion or a few hard feelings.

Agreements are the key to success.

MANY OF US have been programmed to believe that we do not have the power to choose what we want in our lives. We do. Some of us think we cannot move beyond prescribed limits, constraints, and restrictions placed upon us by others. We can. It is often difficult to see the bright side of a difficult situation. It is difficult, not impossible. We are powerful enough to move beyond limits in order to do the impossible, when we choose to. But we have to make the choice.

The law of cause and effect is a fact of life which turns our choices into a reality. Every thought we have leads to a choice. Every word we speak supports choices we make. Every action we take is a choice today which has implications on our tomorrow, next week, and next year. Nothing is impossible tomorrow when we take the time to choose, today. Today, choose to be courageous, rather than fearful. No matter what you face, choose clarity over confusion. Remember to choose discipline over habit; when things are at their worst and when you are at your lowest, choose love over hate or anger. Choices cause a mighty vibration which in effect brings back to us more of what we give out. When we fill our thoughts, words, and deeds with spiritual choices, our days are filled with spiritual light.

Today, I make the choice.

The Valley
of Love

Reminds us that the only relationship we can have
is the relationship we have with the "self."
Everyone else shows us a mirror reflection
of that relationship.

*There are some things wrong with me
that lovin' somebody else won't fix.
When I fix them, I know love
will find me.*

—PHYLLIS HYMAN

YOU DON'T HAVE to meet certain qualifications to be loved. You do not have to do anything special, in a certain way, to get love. The only thing that is ever required of you is to be who you are and feel good about it. Love is not a reward or a prize. Love is not something you can use to trap or be trapped. Love is not even yours to give, nor can it be withheld from you.

Love is the omnipresent flow of life. It is every breath you take. It is the involuntary function of the organs, systems, and parts of your body. Love is your skin, your hair, the way you hold your head, the unique way you laugh or cry and move through the world. Your Creator has never asked you for credentials you don't possess. Anyone who expects more from you than God has a great deal to learn about love.

The love I Am is the love I receive.

WHEN IS IT enough? When is there enough love, enough communication, enough growth, enough satisfaction? In most relationships, there never seems to be enough. Something is missing most of the time, and when it shows up, we want something else.

When the sex is good, the finances are bad. When the finances are in place, the communication is out of whack. Once you start talking to each other, you discover what you don't do, haven't done, and don't have. It will take a great deal of commitment and energy to work together in order to get it together, but you don't have the time. You both have to work to make the money to get more things that will make you feel satisfied.

When is it enough? When are we going to be satisfied with ourselves as whole beings and our mates as unique beings? When will love be enough to inspire us to spend more time just loving and being? When is life and the joy that being alive can bring going to be enough to keep us loving life and living in joy? When is it enough? And, when it's not enough, what do you do about it?

Life is enough! Love is enough! Living life in love is enough!

THE SONG OF Solomon, Chapter 8, Verse 7, reminds us, "Many waters cannot quench love; rivers cannot wash it away." In other words, no matter what happens, love will stand. We often forget this when we are hurt or disappointed by someone we love. We may strike out or say things which we later regret, because under our hurt and anger, there is love. Even when the time comes to end a relationship, under the pain, fear, confusion, there is love.

If you love someone, do not deny it. You can be angry or hurt or even ready to move on, but let the love come through your words and actions. If you are leaving someone, do it with love. Be mindful not to allow shame, guilt, or anger to drown out the love you have shared. If you are being left by someone, stay in love. A departure of the person does not mean the end of love. Like water, love must flow. It changes forms. The tides of love must change. Always remember the way love brought you into a situation, because that same love will get you out of a situation.

The healing flow of love moves through me at all times.

WHAT DOES "MEET me halfway" really mean? When we get halfway, what are we going to do? What lies ahead of us? Who is going to take the first step beyond the halfway point? When someone tells you, "I'm here for you" or "I'll be there for you," what are they talking about? What are you doing there when I'm over here?

One of the biggest problems we face in our relationships is the failure to communicate effectively. We often say things knowing what we mean but without a clear understanding of what the other person has in mind. One of the hindrances to effective communication in a relationship of any kind is the fear that we will ask for too much. We may also be afraid that the other person is unable or unwilling to deliver what we want and need. In the end, you are over here when they are over there, or their half adds up to only one third of your half.

The only way to build strong, stable, mutually satisfying relationships is to be clear. Never be afraid to ask, "What do you mean?" Always be willing to admit, "This is not what I had in mind." Until we make a commitment to communicate clearly and effectively in our relationships, we will be halfway there with nothing happening here.

Clarity in speech brings clear direction.

IT IS ABSOLUTELY amazing that we will talk to strangers in the most polite and patient tones, while we say anything, in any way, to the people we love and care about. We would never speak to the supervisor at work the way we talk to our mates. We rarely say things to unfamiliar children that we frequently say to our own. If company is coming over, we clean up and cook. Yet we have few reservations about stepping over or around the accumulation of clutter that results from daily living.

We must learn to talk to people we love and care about the same way we talk to and treat strangers. We must learn to treat ourselves and loved ones as if we were company. The issue of life is not to impress other people and make them feel good about us. The issue is to develop the kind of character and compassion which allow us to treat ourselves and loved ones in a consistently positive way, based upon the company we are in. When we can do this, we won't spend so much energy switching on and off.

I treat everyone like company.

WHEN YOU ARE feeling down, celebrate your spirit. The essence of life in your body, celebrating your spirit, is celebrating life. The ability to have, to be, and to do is imbedded in your spirit. In this life, we are bound to earth by the physical body. In Spirit, we are bound to the sky, the moon, the stars, the universe, and the Creator. Spirit is the life force of the Creator as it uniquely expresses itself through you! Now, that is something to celebrate!

Celebration of Spirit requires reflection and anticipation. Reflection reminds you of where you've been. Anticipation allows you to keep moving forward. Spirit inspires you to do better, ask for more, expect the best for yourself. Never allow the temporary setback or minor disappointment to dampen the celebration of life. Through Spirit you are divine. In this life, you are Spirit. CELEBRATE WHAT YOU ARE!

Today, I have a reason to celebrate.

DOES IT SEEM that no matter how hard you try, you continue to attract the wrong people as your mate? Perhaps this is because you have forgotten about the Law of Attraction, which states, "What you draw to you is what you are!" We continue to ask life to send us the right person, the person who will make us happy or whole. Under this request is the belief that we are unhappy or not whole. In response, the universe brings us the person and situations to increase what we believe we are. See how it works?

When you focus on what you lack, you receive more of it. When you speak about what you don't want, you create it. The only way to attract and maintain a divine relationship is to be a divine mate. You must be all the things you seek in another person. You must nurture, support, embrace yourself, and you must enjoy your own company. You must be kind to yourself. Generous with yourself. And, most of all, you must love yourself unconditionally. Before you can attract that perfect somebody, you must believe you are the perfect you.

I Am the one I am looking for.

STAYING IN A relationship for economic reasons is not a healthy thing to do. You may be able to convince yourself it's worth it for the money. However, in doing so you put your mental and emotional well-being on the sale rack. When you hang out in an emotionally bankrupt situation, your heart is being condemned in the bargain basement of someone's pocket or bank account.

Sure your checkbook may reflect wealth, but what about your self-worth and self-value? You have placed them on the reject table. Relationships are not like fire sales, where you grab whatever you can for as little as you can. A relationship must be about mutual giving and receiving, where everyone involved is increased in spiritual, emotional, and mental measure.

My heart is not for sale.

IF YOU ARE ending a relationship, be careful not to make food your substitute lover. Eating is an unconscious response that fills the emptiness we feel. We look for something to fill the void and ease the pain. Food always seems to fit the bill. It is painless. It is available. It usually looks, smells, and feels good. Food won't argue with you. It won't take anything from you. It is something you can snuggle up with and settle down with. Food always seems to be there when you need it, but don't let food fool you. It will leave you in much worse shape than your exiting lover.

Instead of a sandwich, ice cream, or pie, try running, dancing, or screaming. If none of that works, find a nice quiet place and cry. You may not feel good when you are doing it, but you will get more out of it than calories, inches, and a body to feel bad about.

Food will not fill the void.

———

I HAVE NEVER been in a relationship that ended when I did not know it was going to end. There were times when I knew long before it ended, and I held on waiting for the axe to fall on my heart. There were other times when I thought it would end, but I stayed and prayed that it wouldn't. I usually forbade myself to think about it. In either case, when the end finally came, I couldn't figure out if I was angry, hurt, or relieved.

By the time we see the trouble in a relationship, it is no longer trouble; it is a disease that has eaten away the core of what the relationship is about. The signs and symptoms have been present for quite a while, but the moment we see them, we fall face-first into denial. We don't want to see or know or hear anything that might confirm what we already know. Women are blessed with a wonderful gift called intuition. It is our safety net. It is like a guardian angel. It is there to protect us and guide us. Unfortunately, it won't work for us unless we pay attention to it!

Know that you know what you know and that it is okay to know! Anything you know is for your own good. Your knowledge will strengthen you. Your knowledge will protect you. Not only will intuitive knowledge open your eyes to see what you need to see; it will also let you know what to do about what you see!

Don't be afraid to see what you know!

IF YOU ARE so willing to be with the wrong person, imagine how wonderful it will be when the right person comes along! In order for that to happen, you must be willing to stop feeling sad, stop being in fear, and stop being in denial. It's not working! That may not be a bad thing.

When a relationship stops working, it usually means that someone has grown. Someone is now ready to receive more and have more than the relationship offers. Someone is ready to be loved, honored, and treated the way they really want to be treated. Could that someone be you? If it is you, that must mean you are ready to say good-bye, ready to dry your eyes, and ready to let go!

Please go, if you must!

A person can love you and still have
developmental problems.
A person can love you while they are plagued by
behavioral deficiencies.
A person can love you and still be
off balance, in denial, or a really bad person.
DON'T TAKE IT PERSONALLY!
Either you love them or you don't!
Either you will stay or you won't!
Make a decision and stick by it!

People do what they do because they do.

ENDING A RELATIONSHIP is never easy, and
telling your partner is going to be a challenge. It
always seems that one person is never ready to let
go when the other one is more than ready. Taking the
unready person's feelings into consideration, the words
never seem to fit. No time seems to be the right time, and
no matter how we do it or when we do it, it is not easy.

When the time comes to end a relationship, here are
a few things you may want to consider: fairness, integrity,
and honesty. It is not fair to yourself or the other person
to stay in a place you do not want to be. You cannot be
your best. You cannot give your best. Forestalling the
good you desire and prolonging the inevitable end also
erodes personal integrity. If you do not feel good about
where you are, you cannot feel good about who you are
there with. You begin to find fault. You lose your sensitiv-
ity. And because of this conflict of emotions, you avoid
speaking the truth about what you feel. Honesty then
becomes the only way out.

Honestly expressing how you feel, as soon as you feel
it, eliminates the tension, anger, and fear that accompa-
nies ending a relationship. Honesty allows you to open
your heart to compassion for the other person without
compromising yourself. In the end, you can make choices
that are fair, from a place in your being that feels good,
while doing what you honestly believe is best for you.

*In all fairness to you and me, I honestly cannot be here
any longer.*

LOVING A CHILD and raising a child are two completely different things. Loving a child means learning how to nurture, teach, and guide. It means being free to let your child know who you are, how you feel, and what you need. Love requires truth, not just sheltering, protecting, or providing. Love means some fun, some pain, some joy, some tears, and absolutely no guarantees.

Raising a child means learning tolerance, patience, acceptance, and forgiveness. It means learning how to teach responsibility, accountability, and dependability. Raising a child requires discipline and obedience, practicing it and teaching it. It means keeping your eyes and your mind open to all things, under all circumstances. Raising a child requires trust, of yourself to do the right thing and of your child to get it . . . eventually.

Many of us love our children so much we forget to raise them. We forget they can see and think and feel. We forget they can fall and get up, with or without our help. We love them because we are afraid to lose them. Yet we lose them because we forget to raise them.

I must love my child enough to raise an adult.

THERE ARE SOME people who come into your life with "WARNING" stamped right in the middle of their forehead. Their story sounds a little strange. Their actions totally contradict their story. You may not know what it is, but you know something is not quite right. What do you do? TRUST YOURSELF!

It is not necessary to have every tidbit of information or to know every gory detail about a person, because your instincts are usually correct. People show you who they are by what they do. If it doesn't feel right, they are probably not! We want to help everybody. Those we can't help, we want to save from themselves. To accomplish this, we will often ignore our natural, self-protective instincts and buy into a sad story. Yes, we want to give everyone the benefit of the doubt, but we also want to learn to trust ourselves.

Learn to trust what your inner voice is telling you. If the person is real, you will find out. Until then, we must stop bandaging bleeding hearts; otherwise, we will continue nursing our grieving hearts.

Nothing ever strikes without warning!

It may seem right now that someone has done something very bad to you. It may strike you that this is unfair; that you don't deserve it; or that it is just downright wickedness on their part. You are probably angry or hurt, or perhaps afraid. You may not understand how or why this has happened. All of this and more may be true about what you feel right now. However, no matter how bad it hurts or how bad you feel, you are not a victim!

Nothing in life happens passively. We are completely responsible for every experience we have, because we determine how we will respond. Sometimes we get stuck in the "Why me?" mode. Life has a way of asking, why not you? If you happen to be in the "I can't help myself" mode, you are available, that's why! Unfortunately, we believe we become victims as a result of what happens, when, in fact, believing we are victims enables things to happen.

Always remember, no matter what is going on in your life, it is your responsibility to choose how you respond. This does not mean you will not hurt. This does not translate to you should ignore what you feel. Not being a victim and taking responsibility means: feel the pain, honor the shock, look for the lesson, and keep on moving in a way that honors who you really are. You are Spirit in a body having a temporary human experience. Your experiences may knock you down, but it is your responsibility not to let them keep you down.

Actively participate in all of your life!

WHEN A MARRIAGE or relationship is about to end, one of the major challenges we must overcome is the belief that we were wrong in choosing the person we are now leaving or losing. No one wants to be wrong, particularly about the person we love. No one wants to admit they gave so much time, energy, or attention to the wrong person or that they did it for the wrong reasons. Often the fear of being wrong will render us dumb or blind to the very thing we must see—the person is no longer right in our lives.

Wrong today does not grow from being wrong yesterday. The person who was absolutely right yesterday may be totally wrong for you today. You have grown, your needs have changed, and there is nothing wrong with that. You are not who you were last year, last month, or last week. You can see with more clarity, feel with greater passion. That does not make you wrong. Nor does it mean you were ever wrong. You were younger, not as smart, a little less prepared, perhaps a bit important. There is nothing wrong with that! There is nothing wrong with you! However, the time has come for you to release what is wrong and make room for what is right.

There is nothing wrong about wanting what is right!

BEFORE YOU GET angry with someone for what they have done, not done, or done to you, honestly ask yourself, "What role did I play in this?" Before you get angry or dismiss the question, honestly ask yourself, Did I say yes when I wanted to say no? Did I say no when I really wanted to say yes? Did I really trust this person? Did I go into the situation in doubt? In fear? Before you start beating up on yourself or anyone else, honestly ask yourself, when did I see this before? When was the last time I was in this place? Feeling this way? Before you give yourself a headache, say something you will be sorry for later, or slump into the valley of depression or anger, honestly ask yourself, "What is the lesson here?"

I know I am learning something!

YOU CANNOT LOSE! It is metaphysically impossible to lose what is meant for you. One reason we stay in relationships we know are going nowhere is because we are afraid of losing something. We think we will lose the person. We feel like we have lost a lot of time. We may even believe we are losing a certain lifestyle or a part of life that has some great meaning to us. What we don't realize is . . . you can never lose!

If the universe intends that you should be with a person, you will be with that person. They may leave. You may leave. However, at the divine time, in the divine way, you will be together. You will have no other choice. If you are with someone and the universe is not in support of the union, there is nothing you can do to keep it together. You must let go! As long as you stay where you are not intended to be, your divine mate cannot get to you. When you let go of what is not working, you will make room for what is going to work. In the end, you haven't lost a thing!

Victory fills all empty places and spaces!

THE PERSON WE love is not a piece of property! They can be a friend, a lover, a husband, or a soul mate. They may be the apple of your eye, the beat of your heart, the crunch in your Cheerios, but they do not belong to you. No matter how much you love them, want them, need them, you will never get them to do what you want, when you want, the way you want. No matter what they say, or what you do, another person cannot belong to you.

A person is a child of God, free to change, able to choose. A person is a being in the process of evolution; flipping and flopping; stumbling and falling; striking out and striking back in order to determine who they are and what they want. We are all little children all grown up. We have toys we want to play with. Fears we want to hide. We may fib to get our way. You can expect a person to say they can when they know that they can't; or to say they will and then forget to do it. A person can be many things you like and even more that you don't. The truth of the matter is, the person in your life is a reflection of you. When you stop trying to own them, you can begin the process of owning up to all parts of yourself.

I will take stock of all of me.

WHEN YOU DO something for someone and their response upsets you, you probably did it for the wrong reason. So what if they didn't say thank you? Why would you expect them to call you? If you put yourself or your finances in peril by doing it, you probably did it for the wrong reason.

It is very easy to convince ourselves that we are doing something for someone when usually the truth is we do it for ourselves. We do it to feel needed and wanted. We do it to make ourselves look better in the other person's eyes. We do things to be noticed. We do other things to take attention away from something we don't want seen. There are instances when we do things because we think we "have to"; we are afraid of what will be said if we don't do it. In each of these instances, we are expecting a certain payoff or payback. If we do not receive it, we become upset with the other person. We believe we've been done, had, ignored, and abused.

We can save ourselves a great deal of grief by doing or giving purely for the joy of doing. With no expectation of reward or return, our giving and doing becomes a blessing to us. It's called service when we serve with joy; the universe, not people, pays us in kind.

I am doing this for the joy of it.

So you've just discovered that your husband, boyfriend, lover has another wife, girlfriend, lover; what do you do? Do you strike out or act out? Do you tell yourself it's not true and continue on as if it is not? The time to figure out what to do is not when it is happening. You must know what you will do before it happens. This knowing is called understanding boundaries.

How you let people into your space will determine how they behave once they get there. How you handle the little things will give you the strength to handle the big things that are bound to come up. We all need boundaries, even in our relationships. We must let people know what is acceptable and what is not, in advance of them stepping across the boundary lines. And we must know what we are willing to do once the line has been crossed.

It is crucial to your own self-worth that you have limits. Those in your life who love you, respect you, and want to be in your space will not risk losing you by crossing the boundary lines. If, for some reason, they choose not to honor your limits, you must do what you said you would do . . . draw the line and don't cross it!

Know in advance what you will and will not accept!

A SELF-RIGHTEOUS WOMAN can drive a man away by demanding perfection. A self-righteous woman actually believes that a man's sole purpose in life is to be what she wants him to be. She may forget that the man is on his own journey through life. She conveniently ignores the fact that men have the same problems, the same issues, and the same fears as most women. Some women have learned to mask their issues much better than men, but that does not give them the right to judge anyone else.

A self-righteous woman can never be satisfied. A man can never live up to her expectations. He can never give enough, do enough, or have enough. Even if he does exactly as he is asked to do, he probably did it too slow or too fast. The one thing a self-righteous woman always overlooks is her own flaws. That is probably why she has so much time to examine the man's shortcomings.

A flawed diamond is still a diamond!

WE ARE USING the wrong math in our relationships. When two people come together to share their lives, 1 + 1 does not equal 2! 1 + 1 = 1! In a relationship, two whole and complete people come together to make a whole and complete union. The parties must be loving, supportive, respectful, and generous to their individual selves before they can offer more of the same to a partner.

Wholeness in this case relates to a healthy sense of self, a wholesome sense of value and worth. Wholeness also means the parties in a relationship each have a sense of direction. Far too often, we use our relationships as a crutch. Something to hold us up. Something which makes it easier to get by. We each want the other person to make us whole. When two cripples try to stand on one crutch, there is a great likelihood that they will both fall down. It is in our own best interest to move in and out of relationships as whole people, with strengths to bring to the table. When we add who we are to who our mate is, we should come up with one wholesome unit.

Seek all that you are in the quest to make it more!

EVERYONE WANTS TO be loved. We seem to know that love heals. Love inspires. Love picks you up, puts a smile on your face, and elongates your spine! We search for love. We wait for it. Some of us are willing to do almost everything to get it. We give up on love, then we give in to love, reaching and groping for the security we believe love will provide for us.

Do you love yourself? Are you in harmony with *you?* Do you treat yourself with respect? Are you generous, kind, and supportive of you? Do you trust yourself and treat yourself as though you can be trusted? Do you accept your weaknesses and celebrate your success? Do you radiate love, or are you just looking to find love and get love? Until you love who you are—not just say it, but do it and believe it—you will never find the love you are or the love you believe someone else has to give you.

The love you are is the love you receive.

ALL RELATIONSHIPS TAKE work. Sometimes that work looks like a disagreement or an argument. It may also look like stress that creates tension. The work may look like a separation. Don't worry! It is all a part of the work. The key to a successful relationship is to allow the work to take place, to allow the communication to continue, and to keep your heart open to love and be loved.

A relationship is not just the place we go to find love, companionship, and intimacy. It is the place we go to heal, to grow, and to work on ourselves. A relationship is an environment which gives us an opportunity to see how much we are capable of giving, how strong we are, and how flexible we can be. The key to successfully working through the issues of a relationship are: to be willing to grow, to be ready to heal, and to keep your heart open to do the work that will be required for your growth and healing.

Love is worth the work.

—————

Glossary of Emotions, Terms, and Spiritual Principles

The terms and principles offered here are from a spiritual or metaphysical (beyond the physical) frame of reference as explanations rather than definitions. In some cases, what is offered may seem to be in conflict/opposition to the intellect, the rational mind, and Webster. For additional research and inquiry, please refer to the following texts:

The Metaphysical Bible Dictionary.
Unity, Unity Village, Unity, MO, 1931.

Charles Filmore: *The Revealing Word.*
Unity, Unity Village, Unity, MO, 1959.

Ernest Holmes: *The Dictionary of New Thought Terms.*
DeVross & Co., Marina Del Rey, CA, 1942.

Acceptance To know that all is well, even when you do not see or understand how it will turn out.

Accountability Considering all actions as creative energy for which you must answer to a Higher Authority.

Affirmation A statement made and accepted as truth.

Aggression Pushing, forcing, moving against the natural, normal, or visible flow.

Alignment   Being in one accord, in harmony and balance with the flow of divine energy.

Anger   The emotional reaction to not having our way, or not having people and events meet our expectations.

Awareness   An inner knowing of divine principles and how they work or manifest in the physical world.

Balance   Having and making time, or spending time and energy attending to all areas and aspects of living/being.

Belief   A mental and emotional acceptance of an idea as being the truth.

Betrayal   When expectations of people and events violate trust given, or when one who is trusted is actively dishonest.

Blame   Giving someone else responsibility for your happiness or well-being. Looking outside of self for the answer or solution.

Blessings   Good fortune which comes your way without any conscious input on your part. The demonstration of God's grace and loving in the physical form.

Celebration   Freedom of the spirit. Giving praise and thanksgiving. Feeling good and demonstrating what you feel.

Challenge   A problematic or difficult situation or experience which arises in the course of life's events. Usually a test of character, spiritual strength, and faith.

Change A shift or movement in the flow of life. The outgrowth of the natural flow of events.

Character The basic essence of the person. What you psychologically and emotionally rely upon, stand upon, look to, hold on to within your self. The foundation of the ability to live.

Clarity A sense of peace, a well-being in the midst of chaos or confusion. The ability to discern the truth within one's own being.

Closure Mental, emotional, and spiritual release. A state of acceptance. Acknowledgment that something which has been a part of your experience no longer exists.

Commitment Unwavering focus. Giving of all one has to offer. Dedication to and faith in a desired course of events.

Compassion The ability to see error without the need to condemn. An open and understanding heart with the ability to offer mercy, truth, and love.

Confinement Mental, emotional, spiritual, or physical impediments to movement, growth, or evolution. A test of spiritual constitution.

Conflict Disharmony. Imbalance. Opposition between forces, energy, or people moving in similar or differing directions. A test of character.

Confusion Mental, emotional, or spiritual darkness. Mental, emotional, or spiritual conflict. Overstimulation of the physical senses.

Consciousness   The total of all ideas accumulated in the individual mind which affects the present state of being. The composite framework of beliefs, thoughts, emotions, sensations, and knowledge which feeds the conscious, subconscious, and superconscious aspects of the individual mind.

Control   Aggression. Conscious attempts to direct the course of events. Unconscious beliefs which stagnate or stymie the course of events. The ability to adjust to the natural flow of events.

Cooperation   The working of one accord, the being in togetherness of two or more forces. Balance, harmony, mutual recognition among forces.

Courage   Freedom from fear. The ability to be, stand, move in the presence of anxiety, danger, opposition. Stepping beyond the mental, emotional, or physical state, the place where one is safe, comfortable, or secure. A test of character.

Death   Spiritual transition from one form to another. The absence of life, whether physical, emotional, or spiritual. Physical dissolution of the body or a circumstance.

Decree   To command with spiritual and emotional authority. Words charged with the power of faith and truth which produce and increase with usage and time.

Denial   Conscious failure or subconscious inability to see, know, or accept truth. As related to affirmations or the spoken word, a denial is the soap and water of the mind which relinquishes a false belief or evil thought.

Depression Unexpressed anger turned inward; feeling burdened or overwhelmed, powerless in the face of situations, unable to have our way.

Desperation A belief in physical, emotional, or spiritual abandonment. Actions taken in denial of truth. Resistance to beliefs of helplessness. Failure to surrender. Relinquishing of faith and trust. A test of character.

Detachment A mental, emotional, and spiritual construct which enables one to withdraw emotional investment in a course of events. The ability to become a witness rather than a participant. Having no mental or emotional attachment to outcome.

Disappointment An emotional construct. Expectations based on false or uncommunicated desires which go unmet. Unfulfilled attachments to the outcome of events.

Discernment "The ability to lay hold of truth." To see beyond appearances to that which is obscure and hidden, but divine.

Discipline Focus. A test of spiritual constitution. The willingness to be taught. The ability to follow through based on faith and obedience.

Diversion Action or activity which attracts one's focus or attention. A conscious or unconscious act taken in response to fear which impedes growth and evolution. A test of character and spiritual constitution.

Divine Mind   The absolute. The Alpha (beginning) and Omega (ending) of creation and life; the unlimited, ever-present, all-knowing, all-powerful Spirit of God.

Doubt   The result of trust and truth being brought into question. Lack of focus and commitment that results in fear. The root of mental and spiritual weakness, leading to indecisiveness. A test of character.

Drama   Active participation in conflict, confusion, and the appearance of that which is false. The attempt to get attention or secure control. Resistance to change. Denial of truth!

Ego   "Easing God out"; seeing our way as the way. Believing we are separate from God. The foundation of fear.

Emotions   Activity of the subconscious mind. Energy within your being that motivates all conscious thought and action.

Empathy   The ability to stand in the circumstances of another and know the truth without judgment. To give to another what one desires for oneself.

Endurance   Unwavering strength grounded in truth and spiritual principles. An outgrowth of courage. The reward of surrender. A test of character.

Evolution   The calling to a higher order. Development achieved by adherence to spiritual law. The unfolding of natural events according to the divinely ordained spiritual plan.

Excitement A lifting or rising up of the consciousness. An expression of good. The prelude to joy. An outgrowth of acceptance.

Faith Spiritual assurance; inner knowing which draws on the power of the heart's desire. Reliance on God's goodness to deliver you from all harm.

Fear False expectations appearing real. Dread, alarm, painful emotion enhanced by the belief in separation. The basic tool of the ego to find fault.

Forgiveness To give up the old for the new, the bad for the good. To allow change to take place. An appeal for healing of the consciousness.

Freedom A mental construct. The ability to know and live the truth. The ability to choose. A state of being without thought of confinement, restraint, limitation, or oppression; having a sense of well-being within which manifests into the outer world.

Grace The omnipresent, omnipotent, all-knowing, perfecting presence of God.

Gratitude Humility of the spirit which gives praise for all. The act of giving praise. The willingness to receive. A test of spiritual discernment.

Greed Insatiable appetite of the physical senses. The absence of gratitude. Belief in lack.

Guilt The belief that there is something profoundly wrong with an act we have committed. A toxic emotion which often leads to shame.

Healing Restoration of the mind, body, or spirit to a

state of Oneness with God. Belief in openness to, receptivity to the presence of God as Spirit.

Helplessness   A mental construct. Failure to recognize truth. Denying the Divine Presence. As it relates to surrender, helplessness is the admission and acceptance of the omnipotence of Spirit.

Honesty   Willingness to know, accept, and promote the truth. The conscious participation in the activation of truth, whether or not it is spoken.

Humility   Making room for the Holy Spirit, God's Spirit, to express through you. The ability to give and serve without expectations of physical reward. Acknowledging God as the giver and doer of all things.

Illumination   Divinely inspired understanding. The ability to see beyond all physical manifestations to the spiritual principle as an active presence.

Impatience   Fear. The absence of faith. The ego's active need to be in control of circumstances and people. A test of character.

Innocence   A childlike state of purity. Pure thought. The outgrowth of forgiveness. The eternal state of spirit.

Inspiration   Divine motivation from within.

Instinct (Sixth Sense)   The voice of Spirit within your consciousness. The presence of the Holy Spirit within the being. (See Intuition.)

Intent   The state of unstated expectation. The cause of all results. The subconscious motivation of all action.

Intuition "Teaching from within." The subconscious and superconscious aspect of the individual mind which brings forth information required for spiritual evolution.

Jealousy Fear. Belief in lack. Manifestation of the lack of self-value, self-worth, and self-love. The ego's need to believe, "I'm not good enough," or "I don't deserve."

Joy The natural expression of the Holy Spirit. A state of well-being and Oneness.

Judgment Fear. A mental construct which involves evaluation by comparison or contrast. The active manifestation of the need to be right. The inability to discern truth.

Justice The effects of spiritual cause. Thought and emotion are the cause of all physical realities. What has been sown in thought and feeling that is reaped through experiences.

Knowledge The scope of information gathered through exposure, experience, and perception. Acquaintance with fact which may or may not be fully reflective of truth. Intellectual knowledge is born of individual mind and subject to judgment. Spiritual knowledge is born of Divine Mind, founded in principle, based on eternal truth.

Lack Fear. A mental and emotional construct. Denial of Divine Presence. The absence of truth.

Limitation A mental construct which gives power to people and conditions. Ignorance of the truth. Relin-

quishing of free choice and free will. An outgrowth
of drama.

Loneliness   A mental and emotional construct based on
the ego's belief in separation and imperfection. Ignorance of stillness, silence, and/or solitude. A test of
spiritual constitution.

Love   In its higher sense: this is the nature of reality. God
is Love. Love is of God. Creates harmony and clarity,
and brings about transformation and unity.

   In its lesser sense: it is an emotional attachment
one has for or shares with another. It comes and goes
depending on one's mood or attitude.

Meditation   The conscious act of stilling the physical
mind. Placing attention on inner communion. Listening within for the voice of Spirit. Cessation of all
outward movement and activity.

Mercy   God's treatment toward those who suffer. Divine
forgiveness which provides a new opportunity.

Mistakes   A natural outgrowth of spiritual evolution.
Confusion between knowledge and truth. An act of
fear based on false perceptions.

Nonresistance—Willingness to acknowledge and honor
the natural flow of events. Relinquishing fear, resentment, and judgment. Fearlessness with a foundation
in trust. The prelude to surrender. A test of character
and spiritual readiness.

Obedience   Unwavering acknowledgment of spirit.
Trust and honoring of self. An outgrowth of discipline. A test of character.

Obstacle   The appearance or manifestation of mental or physical blocks created by one's own thoughts, beliefs, or actions.

Order   The way of the universe. The system of truth by which all things must occur to create harmony.

Pain   Mental, emotional, or spiritual dis-ease. A state of unrest within the consciousness.

Panic   The inevitable outgrowth of disorder and impatience.

Patience   Inner calm in the midst of outer chaos. An act of total surrender to divine order.

Peace   Absolute harmony on all levels: mental, physical, emotional, and spiritual. Unconditional love for all things.

Perseverance   To strive to find truth which brings peace, harmony, and acceptance.

Persistence   Spiritual quality which pushes one on to accomplishment or achievement.

Personal Lies   That which we affirm to ourselves about ourselves and which serves to create belief in lack, restriction, and limitation. A defense mechanism against fear.

Personality   The physical and mental attributes developed in response to environment, experiences, and conditioning, and judgments about the same.

Power   The ability to do.

Praise   Thanksgiving. Conscious acknowledgment and acceptance of the Divine Presence.

Prayer   Communication with and consciousness of the

Divine Presence within the being. The act of communication with the Divine Presence.

Principle Truth in a universal sense as it pertains to God. The orderly working out of truth into expressions or manifestation. The underlying plan by which Spirit moves in expressing Itself. The "I AM" presence within everything living. The formless source which gives birth to all.

Procrastination The act of delaying what one is intuitively afraid to know or experience. A mental and physical defense mechanism against conscious and unconscious fears.

Purpose Actions that are in alignment with the will of God. The underlying cause that sustains all activity in your life. Active pursuit of divine principle as the foundation of your life.

Reality That which is unchanging and eternal. Spiritual presence is the foundation of all real existence; all that is external is an outgrowth of this presence.

Reflection The sum of our thought patterns, beliefs, and actions made manifest in our life, world, and affairs.

Resistance Mental, emotional, or spiritual reversion to the active pursuit of truth. Refusal to humble the spirit. Movement which creates conflict between opposing or complimentary forces.

Respect Conscious regard or consideration for the physical, mental, emotional, and spiritual presence in our world.

Responsibility To be accountable for all that exists and occurs in our lives.

Self-Acceptance Self-knowledge void of criticism and judgment.

Self-Doubt Second-guessing intuitive knowledge. A reflection of low self-worth and self-esteem.

Self-Esteem Healthy regard and beliefs about the self and the ability of the self. Self relating to the inner divinity.

Self-Love Acceptance of all that we are.

Self-Value A high level of regard for self and the desires of the heart. The ability to make the well-being of self a priority in all activities. Divine knowledge of self.

Self-Worth The composite recognition of high self-acceptance and self-esteem. The ability to expect the highest for self and to give the highest of self in all affairs. Recognition of excellence within self.

Service Giving of one's time and resources without expectation of payment or reward. Doing what one is capable of doing for the joy of doing and giving to others.

Shame The belief that something is intrinsically wrong with who you are. A toxic emotion growing out of programming, conditioning, environment, and guilt.

Spirit The substance of life. The supreme energy of Mind. Life, power, and the activity of truth. The Father/Mother principle that creates and sustains all life.

Spirituality   A state of thought which directly links the mind to the one Creative Cause of life. A state of consciousness that grows and unfolds through disciplined activity that relates to Spirit. The active awareness and acknowledgment of the presence of Spirit. (Spirit when capitalized is a name for God.)

Stillness   See Peace.

Surrender   Psychological and emotional release. Acknowledgment of the power of spiritual activity. Obedience to spiritual principle which evolves into an experience of peace and well-being. An act of acceptance.

Temptation   A proving or testing of your will, character, or faith. An adversarial force which causes one to question or hold on to spiritual beliefs and principles.

Transformation   Change within the form, structure, condition, or nature of your being. A shift in consciousness resulting in the release of false ideas and beliefs.

Trust   Unquestioning belief and fearless expectation in the operation of divine law and order. Mental and emotional commitment to the will of God.

Truth   An aspect of God that is Absolute and encompassing. The foundation of spiritual principle. That which is in accord with the divine principle of God as the creative source and cause. The immutable, everlasting word that is now, has been, will ever be eternally consistent.

Understanding Comprehension of truth and Spirit principle. Integration of intellectual and spiritual knowledge.

Wisdom Intuitive knowing and spiritual intuition. The voice of God within the being as the source of understanding and action. The ability to act in accordance with knowledge and principle.

Index